TAXI TALES
FROM PARIS

D1614542

NICKY GENTIL

Matador
9 Priory Business Park,
Wistow Road, Kibworth Beauchamp,
Leicestershire. LE8 0RX
Tel: 0116 279 2299
Email: books@troubador.co.uk
Web: www.troubador.co.uk/matador
Twitter: @matadorbooks

ISBN 978 1838592 370

British Library Cataloguing in Publication Data.
A catalogue record for this book is available from the British Library.

Printed and bound by CPI Group (UK) Ltd, Croydon, CR0 4YY
Typeset in 12pt Minion Pro by Troubador Publishing Ltd, Leicester, UK

Matador is an imprint of Troubador Publishing Ltd

For my husband Etienne, who good-naturedly indulges my increasing inclination to take taxis when public transport will indeed do!

About the Author

In 1988, fresh out of Oxford University with a degree in French and German, Nicky Gentil moved to Paris to pursue a career in translation.

Some twenty years later – having acquired a husband and two children along the way! – she took up jazz improvisation on the piano, rapidly discovering a great passion for it, so much so that, in 2016, she published a book on the subject. Her first published work, *La jazz-girl passionnée et son dévoué accordeur* (Éditions Beaurepaire), is a light-hearted, feel-good account of her unexpected road to jazz.

The book received an overwhelmingly positive response at France's 2016 EuroPiano Congress. Consequently, at the suggestion of the English-speaking attendees and in light of numerous requests from family and friends in the UK, she translated her work into English. It was published in March 2018 under the title *The Jazz-Girl, the Piano, and the Dedicated Tuner* (Matador Publishing).

In October of that same year, she also published *Petits dialogues en taxi* (Éditions Beaurepaire) – a collection of around thirty tales recounting some of her more memorable cab rides since moving to France – in celebration of her thirtieth anniversary in the capital.

Taxi Tales from Paris is the English version of that work.

Today, Nicky Gentil divides her time between her writing, translating her writing and her various musical activities.

CONTENTS

PROLOGUE

It was actually an American writer who gave me the inspiration for this collection of tales… although he is blissfully unaware of it!

In 1995, having just been entrusted by *The New Yorker* with the somewhat enviable task of writing a series of essays on all aspects of life in France, Adam Gopnik relocated to Paris – together with his wife and young son – for a period of five years.

Gopnik's essays were subsequently grouped together in a book – the poetically titled *Paris to the Moon* – that shot into the bestseller lists when it came out in the States in the year 2000.

One of the many reasons I so love *Paris to the Moon*, to the extent that I tend to recommend this work as a kind of indispensable 'bible' to any English-speaker who comes to live here in the French capital, is because I can really relate to it. The sense of pure wonderment that life in Paris elicits from this American author, reminds me so much of my own when first I moved here over thirty years ago. Indeed, a single binding thread lies at the heart of Gopnik's fascinating narrative relating the widely differing events that marked his five-year stay, such as the general strike of 1995, the trial of the Nazi war-criminal Maurice Papon, and the spectacularly elegant way in which France's *Grande Dame* – aka the Eiffel Tower – saw in the year 2000, to name but a few. It is a thread of undiluted praise for literally *every* aspect of his new environment: the stunning architecture, the fine food, not to mention the wonderful light of the 'most beautiful city in the world', including that more sombre 'grey-violet' light of the seemingly endless, sun-deprived winter days!

Furthermore, Gopnik does not limit his undiluted praise exclusively to the grandiose. As if being in Paris serves to re-awaken each and every one of his senses, he also happily lingers over descriptions of the more simple pleasures arising from his new-found way of life: the joy, for example, of sipping *un express* (the French word for espresso) in his favourite local café, or that of being able to obtain a hot and crusty freshly-cooked baguette every evening on his way home. In short, he is bowled over by all those little 'treats' that actually constitute the norm for the average French man or woman, but are generally considered, by the vast majority of foreigners who come to this country, to be a source of pure delight.

Having said that, in spite of all Gopnik's reactions to which I can so relate, ultimately if I had to choose just one reason for loving his book it would be this: towards the end comes a truly memorable passage recounting *the* most unlikely of conversations with a Parisian cabdriver; so unusual is this exchange that I can still recall it to this day – many years after having read about it – as if I discovered it only yesterday.

To give you the context, Gopnik's wife, Martha, is at the time pregnant with their second child. This happy state of affairs provides Gopnik with a convenient opportunity to devote an entire essay to the subject comparing the different approaches between France and the States, or more precisely Paris and New York. And, once again, the American author is pleasantly surprised by his Parisian experience, as evidenced by his descriptions of the 'wonderful' health service, the 'luxury' – afforded to any woman who has just given birth – of being able to stay in hospital for four or five days in order to rest and have time to bond with her newborn, and the cool elegance of the obstetricians who in Gopnik's world all seem to sport the same 'uniform' of black jeans and matching roll-neck sweater – a far cry from the traditional white coat of his expectations!

At the same time, he is genuinely amused, as is his wife, when the doctor advises, half-way through the second term of the pregnancy, that Martha should do some sport – swimming for example – because he considers she has put on far too much weight. In the case in point, she has put on just half the amount gained at the same stage of her first pregnancy when she lived in the States!

Naturally, as one would expect, Martha's pregnancy also gives this couple an opportunity to learn a whole new set of French expressions, one of which stands out head and shoulders above the rest. Whenever they announce that they are expecting a baby girl, the response – given that they already have a son – is systematically the same: '*Ah, c'est le choix du Roi!*' In other words, in the eyes of the French, they are in the process of hitting some kind of parental jackpot apparently known to all as 'the king's choice'; without exception everybody, literally everybody – the doctor, the neighbours, the security guard in their block of flats, the local baker, the butcher etc. – says it.

And then there's the cabdriver…

One day, taking heed of the doctor's advice, the family decides to go to the swimming pool. According to Gopnik, their cabdriver, dressed in an old pair of ripped jeans, a short-sleeved shirt and displaying a row of metal where his teeth would normally be, does not exactly bring to mind your typical intellectual.

And yet…

The cabdriver begins the conversation by profusely congratulating the couple's young son on his fluent French, spoken with absolutely no trace of an accent. Then, alluding to Martha's condition, he asks them:

'So, is your little boy about to have a baby brother or a baby sister?'

Together they chorus:

'A baby sister.'

At this point Gopnik grimaces. He knows what's coming. It's inevitable. They are about to hear THE expression – the one and only response to their happy news – in Gopnik's eyes, a monotonous refrain of which he is growing increasingly weary. Thus it is that he braces himself for the exclamation that naturally comes bang on cue.

With a slap on the steering wheel, the cabdriver triumphantly declares:

'*Ah, c'est le choix du roi!*'

Gopnik is by now so fed up of hearing this that he murmurs: '*Please* explain it to me.' It is said ironically, rhetorically almost, but the cabdriver doesn't miss a beat as he parks his car in order to be able to give his passengers the following mini-history lesson:

'In Latin countries we have what we call Salic law, which means that only your son can inherit the throne… a French king, under Salic law, had to consolidate his hold on the throne by having a boy. And he had to have a girl, so that she could be offered in marriage to another king, and in this way the royal possessions would be expanded since the daughter's son would be a king too.'

As Gopnik sits there in silence, the cabdriver expands:

'It is very odd because in the Hundred Years' War the King of England, as Duc de Guyenne, a title he had inherited from his grandfather, was subject to Salic law too. The story of how this worked itself out in the making of the two monarchies is a passionately interesting piece of history. I recommend the series *Les Rois Maudits* (the dammed or cursed kings), which is a fascinating study of this history, particularly of the acts of John the Good and what he did as an act of policy to accommodate the Salic principle. The books are by Maurice Druon of the *Académie Française*, and I heartily recommend them. Passionately interesting.'

This explanation leaves Gopnik and his wife utterly speechless for the rest of their journey!

Often, when taking a taxi, I will think of this quite remarkable scene. And maybe I'm mistaken but I simply cannot imagine having this type of exchange with a London or New York cabdriver. Whenever I recount this anecdote to English-speaking friends who live here they too are of the same opinion. 'It could only happen in France' is the unanimous reaction. And, just to be clear, it is always said in a positive, admiring tone.

So, you see, it is for this reason that for many years I would muse – without actually acting upon it – about how some of the more memorable conversations I've had with cabdrivers since moving here, over thirty years ago, could make a great subject for a book.

*

While it did indeed take another man's cab ride to give me the inspiration for this collection of tales, on the other hand it took another cab ride altogether – many, many years after having discovered Adam Gopnik's – for me to actually put pen to paper...

It happened one Sunday afternoon in October.

That day, my husband and I had tickets for a recital by a French pianist who is particularly dear to our hearts. In spite of this, we were really dragging our heels. At the time, the whole of France was enjoying an absolutely spectacular Indian summer. Consequently, we had no wish to prise ourselves away from our terrace, where we had just had lunch, and where we were sorely tempted to spend the rest of the afternoon lazing around, a-reading and a-snoozing.

Be that as it may, neither of us wanted to waste the tickets – booked some months previously and coveted by many – and we both agreed that once we got to the recital we would be happy to have made the effort.

Before setting off, in accordance with our personal family tradition, we had some serious negotiating to do: I wanted to go there by taxi while my husband was all for taking the *métro*. For ecological reasons, my better half will use public transport whenever he can and I cannot deny that he is absolutely right to do so. From a purely selfish point of view, however, the idea of spending an hour in a jam-packed *métro*, in the scorching heat of that particular afternoon, did not exactly appeal to me. We thus did a deal: we'd take a taxi to go there on the condition we use public transport to come home.

The journey took about half an hour, during which our cabdriver – seeing that we were happily dozing in the back – barely spoke to us, choosing instead to save the best for last.

Thus it was that, upon arriving at our destination, he immediately leapt out of the car, raced round to the side so that he could open the door for me and then, as I alighted, shook my hand!

Finally he gave me an explanation, one that took me even further aback than his most considerate gestures.

'*Madame*, I would just like to take this opportunity to express my immense gratitude towards you. Thanks to you, I have completely given up smoking.'

The effect of his words was immediate – as if he'd pushed some kind of mental button that was now raising numerous questions in my head *all* at the same time. What on earth was he talking about? Where had I met him? What could I possibly have done to have such a huge influence on his personal habits? Had I – heaven forbid – been rude to him? Etc., etc…

In response to my perplexed look, he added:

'Last summer, I dropped you and your daughter off at the airport.'

The penny finally dropped as his words transported me back in time to the month of July…

*

I felt as if I were suffocating – both physically and mentally. The heat in Paris was punishing. Added to that was the prospect of a difficult weekend. I was going to England with my daughter in order to help my siblings move our mother into a retirement home, and I was really dreading the days ahead. It was the end of an era for everybody.

As I got in the taxi that day, the pungent stench of cigarette smoke merely served to intensify my feelings of suffocation, inciting me to open the windows, which in turn incited the cabdriver to say to me:

'*Madame*, it's really very hot today. Wouldn't you rather shut the windows so I can put the air-conditioning on?'

Not wishing to offend him I kept my reply to a strict minimum, content to utter a mere: 'No, thank you.'

A few minutes later, the cabdriver pursued the matter with:

'*Madame*, there really is no air in Paris today. It would be so much better if you were to shut the windows so that I can put the air-conditioning on.'

Now I didn't have a choice. I was going to have to explain the problem, which I attempted to do diplomatically:

'I'm sorry to say this but your car really smells of smoke. Maybe it was the previous clients but if you close the windows the smell will be unbearable.'

Unfortunately, any attempt at diplomacy on my part turned out to be counterproductive as the cabdriver replied:

'No, *Madame*, I'm the one who's sorry. It can't be the previous clients because smoking in taxis is strictly prohibited. That's also why I never smoke in my car. I always take a break and get out to have a cigarette. However, it would appear that my suit must have absorbed some of the smoke.'

By now I was mortified so I attempted to defuse the situation by taking some of the blame:

'I'm so sorry to have mentioned it. Truly, I am. But you see... well, the thing is, I have never smoked in my entire life and this makes me extremely sensitive to the smell. Unfortunately, there's nothing I can do about it. So, if you don't mind, I'd like to leave the windows open, at least until we reach the ring road. Then, I agree, it would probably be better to close them.'

Who would have thought it? There I was, on this beautiful October day, standing opposite the very same cabdriver who was now about to tell me precisely what had happened, subsequent to my previous journey with him:

'Your comments about the pungent smell in my car had a really devastating effect on me. I remember telling you how careful I was, how I would always get out of the car to smoke. But until I had you as a client I just didn't realise that, even though I thought I was taking the necessary precautions, my car could stink so much! You've no idea how ashamed I was. That said, though, you really did the right thing by pointing it out to me because since that day I have not smoked a single cigarette. It was utterly radical! As a result of your comments I stopped smoking, literally overnight. And for that I cannot thank you enough.'

'It's really nice of you to tell me that. I do indeed remember feeling absolutely mortified by our conversation that day. However, since it had such a positive consequence, now I don't regret it at all.'

Barely had we left the cabdriver when I turned to my husband and said:

'I totally agree that it makes sound ecological sense to use public transport. That said, here's one *extremely* good reason to take taxis: I always have *the* most surprising conversations with cabdrivers. Well, perhaps not always. But over the years, I've had some pretty memorable ones! And that's precisely why I've been thinking for some time now that they could make a really great subject for a book. One day, maybe…'

*

The piano recital lasted about an hour and, ultimately, we were really pleased we'd forced ourselves to abandon our sun-drenched terrace. In fact, so transported was I by the music that I even forgot my most surprising conversation with the cabdriver.

Or so I thought…

To this day, I would be quite incapable of explaining just what it was about that particular cab ride that galvanised me. What I can say, though, is this: that night my subconscious must have set to work, very hard indeed. And the consequence was crystal clear.

The next morning, in the space of two hours, this book literally 'wrote' itself in my head.

Naturally, it took me somewhat longer to put everything down on paper.

What follows is the result…

THE CARICATURE

In June 1987, having just completed a four-year degree course in modern languages, it was with one single goal in mind that I left university. My dream was to pursue a career in translation, but not just anywhere. I wanted to work in Paris.

The road to fulfilling this dream was a little long; in those pre-Internet days, devoid of Skype and communication by email, applying for a job abroad was somewhat more complicated than it is today.

Better late than never, however. Having spent a year surviving financially thanks to a combination of some freelance translation, lots of babysitting and the occasional temping assignment, I finally managed to obtain a much coveted – at any rate, by me! – translation job in the French capital.

I don't think I shall ever forget the day I got that job. My temping assignment of the moment, for a major property company based in central London, saw me working in a massive open-plan office. And when I announced my good news, the screams of 'congratulations' ran from one end of this huge open space to the other in what I can only describe as the verbal equivalent of a truly amazing Mexican wave! Everybody knew just how much I had been dreaming of this job and, that day, they were all eager to share in my unbridled joy.

*

city of Paris, *not* the suburb, and is therefore displaying an amount that is way too low for this journey!'

With my life currently in this angry man's hands, naturally I sought to defuse the situation, making him an offer that was – in my humble opinion – most generous:

'I completely understand how annoying this must be for you. And let's face it anyone can make a mistake. So, why don't you tell me what this journey should really be costing me and I'll pay you that amount, instead of the amount displayed on the meter, when you drop me off.'

Bizarrely, my kind offer only served to make him angrier as he exclaimed:

'But I've no way of knowing, *putain!* It varies considerably, from journey to journey.'

Now at a complete loss for words, I remained silent until the taxi pulled up in front of my building.

Alighting from the car, I then handed an amount to the cabdriver that was substantially more than that displayed on the meter, still clinging onto the belief that my gesture would appease him. Sadly, though, there was nothing for it. Upon counting the money, he practically spat out another really angry '*Putain!*' to which I replied:

'Don't overdo it, now. I'm trying hard to be generous with you. I'm under no obligation to add anything to the amount displayed. But I'm doing it anyway, to help make up for your mistake.'

My words did little to calm him down. Quite the opposite in fact!

'But you're forgetting the suitcase. *Putain!*'

The rule has long since changed but, in those days, cabdrivers used to charge a supplement for suitcases. However, since at the time I rarely travelled anywhere by taxi, I had absolutely no way of knowing this. Consequently, my 'generous' increase was actually anything *but* in the eyes of the cabdriver. As I subsequently found out, all I had added was in fact the mere equivalent of the additional amount owed for my luggage!

All of a sudden this scene taking place before me, in the street in the middle of the night, with, as its main player, a man who was the *very* caricature of every description I had ever heard of aggressive, stressed-out Parisians, struck me as quite ridiculous. To the extent that I could not help but burst out laughing which, as far as my cabdriver was concerned, was evidently the worst thing I could possibly do.

With his already high level of anger seriously on the rise, in response he grabbed my suitcase and tossed into it the street before screaming out one last '*PUTAIN DE MERDE!*' for the road!

∗

Luckily, this type of exchange with Parisian cabdrivers – however 'entertaining' it may be – occurs only very rarely.

On that note, I now invite you to discover the tale of a somewhat more amusing cab ride…

THE TEASE

I live on an avenue in the sixteenth arrondissement of Paris. Well 'avenue' is in fact saying a lot because in reality the road is quite narrow – just fourteen yards – and only two hundred and sixty yards long. To put it in perspective, that avenue generally referred to by foreigners and Parisians alike as 'the most beautiful avenue in the world' – in other words the *Champs-Elysées* – measures seventy-six yards wide and some two thousand and eighty yards long!

Be that as it may, it is not so much the (in my view inappropriate) term of 'avenue' that poses a problem as the actual name of the street itself, because, as luck would have it, this name sounds very much like that of another avenue in the exact same arrondissement. Furthermore, this 'other' avenue happens to be genuinely worthy of the term because it is much bigger and, above all, extremely well known. The real thing, if you will.

For the purposes of this tale, let's imagine, that my avenue is called the *Camps-Elysées*. Do you see the problem now?

Over the years, I have observed that whenever I take a taxi to go home, the conversation can go one of two ways.

Conversation A goes something like this:

'You want to go to the *Camps-Élysées*? Sorry, never heard of it! The *CHAMPS-Elysées*, now there's an avenue that everybody knows. But the *Camps-Elysées*, well, frankly, I don't know what you're talking about...'

6

Traditionally, at this point, the cabdriver will look at me as if I'm some kind of madwoman! After all, EVERYBODY has heard of the *Champs-Elysées*, haven't they? So how could anyone possibly get this name wrong?

This is my cue to convince the cabdriver that I know exactly what I'm doing by giving the following details:

'I'm quite sure you do know the avenue to which I'm referring. It starts at the crossroads of street X and goes all the way up to avenue Y.'

'*Mais oui!* Of course I know that avenue. I know it well. I take it almost every day. So that's what it's called? *Avenue des Camps-Elysées!* Really? Well, well, well! You learn something every day. And today, you've really enlightened me. So thank you. Thank you very much. *Avenue des Camps-Elysées* it is then.'

Conversation B, on the other hand, goes like this...

I get in the taxi, announce my address, and the cabdriver sets off without questioning it.

I therefore have to check that he's understood correctly:

'*Monsieur*, can I just make sure we're clear on this? I want to go to the *Camps-Elysées*.'

'Yes, yes, I know you do. I heard you. You want to go to the *Champs-Elysées*.'

At this point, I risk offending the cabdriver – who is already sorely tempted to add something along the lines of 'Are you trying to tell me how to do my job?' – because I am now obliged to insist, emphasising the name of a destination that, as far as he is concerned, does not require any emphasis whatsoever! And that is why, here, it is wise to proceed as tactfully as possible:

'That, *Monsieur*, is precisely my point. I'm NOT going to the *Champs-Elysées*. The reason I want to make sure you've understood the exact name of my avenue is because it really is called the *CAMPS-Elysées*. Do forgive me for pointing this out. I'm merely trying to prevent you from making a classic mistake.'

Conversation B can now continue, in much the same way as conversation A, to conclude with:

'*Mais oui!* Of course I know this avenue. I know it well. I take it almost every day... etc.'

Since I have lived at the same address for a good ten years now, every time I take a taxi home the conversation is practically a reflex, as if the sentences are pre-programmed in my mind. All I have to do is press a mental button – A or B according to how the cabdriver reacts upon hearing my address – and the set phrases pop out without my even needing to think about it. It's always like that.

Well almost...

One day, when, upon hearing the name of my avenue, the cabdriver remained silent and just started driving, naturally I thought we must be going for Conversation B.

I thus pulled out the appropriate stock question:

'*Monsieur*, can I just make sure we're clear on this? I want to go to the *Camps-Elysées*.'

To my surprise, the cabdriver's response was again one of silence.

Somewhat taken aback, in a bid to obtain any kind of verbal reaction, I now decided to volunteer a mere:

'*Monsieur?*'

But the response remained steadfastly the same. Silence. This time, deafening.

Well, if that's how it's going to be, let's go with silence, I thought to myself.

And that is how this particular cab ride started – with me feeling rather irritated. After all, I had taken the necessary precautions to ensure my cabdriver did not fall into the classic trap. So now all I had to do was sit back and let him get on with it. And if he did go to the wrong street, the mistake would be on him.

That day, however, there was no mistake. On the contrary, I was surprised to see that the cabdriver was going the right way without requiring any directions at all from me.

It turned out there was a very good reason for this.

As the taxi approached the crossroads that marks the beginning of my avenue with the problematic name, the red traffic light could not have come at a better moment. The fact that the cabdriver had to stop the car meant that he was now perfectly placed to savour the delicious moment. Delicious, that is, as far as he was concerned!

Turning to me, with a massive teasing grin on his face, he said:

'*Madame*, I happen to know this avenue VERY well indeed.'

'Really?'

'REALLY!'

'How is that?'

'You see that building just there?'

The building he was pointing to was the very first one, number one in fact, on my avenue.

'Well, the thing is, that's where I was born! There. Just opposite. In that very building! So, you see, how could I possibly not know this particular avenue?'

Thrilled to have scored such an amazing point, the cabdriver was unable to contain his smile – a smile so wide that it spread from ear to ear, rendering it clearly visible even from where I was seated in the back of the car. It was, moreover, a persistent smile for it remained firmly on his face right until the moment he pulled up in front of my building.

That put me in my place!

ANOTHER TEASE!

I t was a good while before I realised that the cabdriver was going in completely the opposite direction of where I needed to be. Worse still, it was *all* down to my poor instructions.

Without further ado I explained my mistake, whereupon the cabdriver could not resist having a little 'I told you so' moment:

'And yet, you must admit, I did ask you if you were *absolutely* sure.'

By way of an apology, I tried to make light of it:

'I know. I'm sorry. But what can you do? It's well known that we women have no sense of direction. We may have many other truly great qualities but, sadly, we don't have that one.'

The cabdriver, however, managed to go one better.

'What? You women? No sense of direction? Are you kidding me? On the contrary, I'd say you all have highly developed skills in that department! *Especially* when it comes to relationships – a fine example, if ever there was one, of how the female species tends to do all the directing! Wouldn't you agree?'

Now how could I possibly argue with that?

THE BEGINNER

S ometimes, I come across a cabdriver who is just starting out. Obviously, everyone needs to start somewhere. The tale that follows, however, clearly demonstrates that there are beginners and, well… beginners!

✶

Our cabdriver's response to the name of our destination – *la rue Saint-Louis-en-l'Île* – situated in the heart of Paris and known to all, was most unexpected:

'Where's that?'

Acknowledging the look of surprise on our faces, he added:

'I'm so sorry. It's my first day.'

My husband, being not only *Gentil* by name but also *gentil*[3] by nature, immediately proceeded to put him at ease by replying:

'Don't worry. Everyone needs to start somewhere. But you'll see, it's really easy. It's the street that goes right down the middle of the Île *Saint-Louis*.'

'Where's that?'

This left my husband speechless. So I decided to take over:

'Well, that's really easy too. The *Île Saint-Louis* is just behind *Notre Dame Cathedral*.'

---

3   *Gentil* : French for kind or nice

Sadly, in spite of our best efforts to help this young beginner, his answer came back, for the third time, in the form of exactly the same question:

'Where's that?'

No comment.

Postscript

Having ended this particular tale with the words 'No comment', I now feel inclined to do just the opposite because translating this piece from my original French manuscript turned out to be a particularly poignant exercise for me. I wrote the English version just one week after watching in horror – like countless other people – as Notre Dame Cathedral *was engulfed and considerably ravaged by flames.*

On that fateful night, the smoke drifted in a southwesterly direction towards the Eiffel Tower. Consequently, in addition to seeing the catastrophe unfurl before my eyes on the television, I was able to observe its very trace from our window, the grey hues slowly but surely – insidiously almost – forming an ugly scar across what would have otherwise been a beautiful spring sky, thereby obliterating the glorious scarlet tones of the sunset.

News reporters were keen to point out precisely why it was so very devastating to see this particular monument in flames. On top of its huge religious significance for the Catholic community, it was a major tourist attraction receiving a staggering thirteen million visitors every year. Then there were the numerous, irreplaceable works of art; people were saddened by the fact that anything destroyed would signify the disappearance of a tangible link with the past, forever.

For many, myself included, a further detail made this scene utterly gut wrenching. Notre Dame Cathedral *happens to be the official, geographical centre of Paris; set in the paving stones in front of this majestic edifice is a plaque indicating what is known as 'Le point zéro' because it is from this precise spot that the distance from the capital to all other French towns is measured. So, you see, when the Cathedral began to burn down, it was in fact the city's centre, its heart and soul, that was on fire.*

To return to the subject of my taxi tale, Notre Dame's 'official city centre' status makes the novice cabdriver's questions all the more surprising. Obviously, our encounter occurred before the advent of the GPS. However, there was – and still is – a rather stringent test to pass in order to be able to take on the job of cabdriver in Paris, similar to that which requires would-be London cabdrivers to acquire 'The Knowledge'. Yet here was a cabdriver who claimed not to know the location of a landmark as significant to Paris as Big Ben is to London.

Conclusion: we will never know how long this young man survived in his chosen profession but I suspect 'not very' would be the short answer to that!

THE CABDRIVER
WHO SURPRISED ME!

My sister once said:
'I do wish someone would invent the equivalent of that music App Shazam for foreign languages.'

I know what she means because every time I hear a foreign language that is unfamiliar to me (in other words the vast majority given that our world boasts an impressive number of around seven thousand different languages!), I like to try to identify it, or at least place it on the appropriate continent. So much so that, over the years, this has turned into a guessing game that my husband and I will often play when we are in a public place. It is a game at which my better half appears to excel.

Recently, for example, we were in a restaurant where we found ourselves seated near a couple who were clearly speaking a Northern European language. While my husband was convinced it was Finnish, I was definitely going with Swedish.

By the end of the evening, our curiosity getting the better of us, we decided to put the question to them, only to discover that they had indeed been speaking Finnish. This caused me to say:

'You know, it's always my husband who wins! I was convinced you were speaking Swedish, but he got it right.'

To my surprise, however, the woman added:

'Actually, you're not entirely wrong. My husband is Swedish. And even though he talks to me in Finnish, he always uses a lot of Swedish words.'

So, in a way, we had in fact both been right; conjugal peace and harmony was thus preserved. Phew!

Having said that, my basic point here is the following: if there is one foreign language that I systematically fail to recognise, it generally turns out to be Portuguese...

*

The cabdriver had just spent a good ten minutes on the phone speaking a language of which every aspect – intonation, rhythm, and syllables alike – was completely and utterly unfamiliar to me. So logically, in the face of such a verbal mystery, my guess should have been that it was Portuguese. But here's the thing: never before had I encountered a man with such jet-black skin. (*Allow me, before I go any further, to be perfectly clear on this: my reference to the colour of the cabdriver's skin is a purely objective observation and in no way a racist comment.*) I therefore deduced – nothing gets past me (!) – that my cabdriver must hail from Africa, which incited me to put the following question to him:

'*Monsieur*, I hope you don't mind my asking but, just out of curiosity, what language were you speaking on the telephone?'

'Ethiopian.'

'Ah, thank you. You know it's a funny thing but when literally every aspect of a language seems unfamiliar to me, when I don't recognise anything at all, not so much as a single syllable or sound, then generally it turns out to be Portuguese. But there you go, I've just found a second language that has exactly the same effect on me.'

Imagine my surprise when the cabdriver replied:

'Actually, *Madame*, you're not far wrong. The Ethiopian language is in fact very similar to Portuguese.'

'Really?'

'Yes. Really. It's all due to a war that took place, back in the sixteenth century, between the Sultanate of Adal and my country. After twenty years of fighting, Ethiopia won in 1543 but only because we had the support of what was then the Kingdom of Portugal. And this left a trace. The Portuguese troops had a major influence on our language that remains to this day.'

Well, who would have thought it?

THE SINGING CABDRIVER

My husband and I were on our way to the airport and, since it was rush hour, looked set to be spending a rather long time in the taxi. This wasn't a problem in itself – we'd left ourselves plenty of time to get there. But there was, nevertheless, a hitch: as he negotiated the dense traffic our cabdriver seemed bent on singing the same three bars of music, over and over again.

Rolling my eyes to heaven, I turned to my husband and whispered in English so the cabdriver wouldn't understand: 'Oh God, I sincerely hope we don't have this on a loop all the way to Charles de Gaulle', at which point, the cabdriver miraculously stopped and then, said to us:

'You know, it's a funny thing, I hardly ever pick up clients in this part of Paris but, a couple of days ago, last Saturday evening in fact, I picked up two girls from your very building who were going to a party at the Palais de Tokyo.'

Grinning at my husband, I feigned ignorance as I asked the cabdriver:

'Oh really. Is that so? And what were they like?'

'Amazing. I had the two most beautiful girls you could wish to meet in my cab. They were so elegantly dressed and extremely polite, utterly charming too. Do you know them?'

'We do.'

'Are they neighbours of yours?'

'Well, yes, in a manner of speaking you could say one of them is a neighbour, in the sense that she does indeed live in our building. In fact, she lives in our flat. You see, the thing is, she happens to be our daughter. The other one is her best friend.'

'Well, you both have good reason to be proud. So do the parents of her best friend. The girls were lovely.'

By now we were indeed overflowing with parental pride. So much so that I immediately grabbed my phone and texted the mother of our daughter's best friend so that she too could cherish the moment.

I then texted our daughter, to tell her that we had the very same cabdriver she'd had the previous Saturday, who mischievously wrote back:

'*Oh dear, is he singing?* ☺ '

I was just about to reply: 'No, thank God. He stopped to tell us all about you two,' when bang on cue he started humming the same three bars of music again and continued to do so right up until the moment he dropped us off.

But, no matter, when you're a proud parent you can put up with an awful lot from the person who has just reminded you precisely why you should be!

MORE MUSICAL TALES...

'Our role as parents is to teach our children to play the piano of life. After that it is up to them to live their lives in harmony, according to the melody of their choice.'

These highly poetic words were spoken by the cabdriver of the French classical pianist Claire-Marie Le Guay as he drove her to the Steinway factory in Hamburg where she was due to perform a recital on Mozart.

The cabdriver's name was none other than Wolfgang!

*

Traditionally, the decade of our forties goes hand in hand with the term 'mid-life crisis'. In my case, however, the word 'explosion' would be so much more appropriate...

For many years I had been quietly tootling along in life, slowly but surely ticking off the boxes of my ambitions – university, career, marriage, children – thereby reaching fairly standard, traditional milestones that were, nevertheless, terribly exciting to me. Consequently, I was happy, fulfilled, in search of nothing... at least not consciously.

Then, one day, boom!

I was indeed well into my forties when jazz literally 'exploded' into my life, rapidly going on to become a GREAT passion of mine; with the completely unexpected arrival of this most precious of treasures, my existence thus metamorphosed forever.

Today, music is so essential to my daily life that inevitably a large number of my conversations with cabdrivers revolve around this subject.

The two that follow are my favourites…

The Appreciative Cabdriver

On that particular 23rd December – the day I reached my half century on this planet – one word, and one word alone, would have sufficed to describe my state of mind: euphoric!

And yet, I spent a large part of this day in a bunker...

In celebration of this milestone birthday, my husband had found a great present for me: an afternoon of jazz lessons with my favourite French pianist of all time, that veritable genius of improvisation – Fabrice Eulry.

At the time, I did not know Fabrice personally; I had merely become familiar with his work through his shows. Be that as it may, my better half had taken it upon himself to contact Fabrice in secret and this exceptional, completely 'off the chart' (in terms of talent) pianist had immediately agreed to give me an afternoon of lessons. Hence my euphoria. What a privilege to be able to work with THE Fabrice Eulry! And what better example could there be of this truly great artist's generosity than to have accepted me – a mere beginner in jazz – as his pupil?

It was early afternoon when I arrived at Fabrice's home where his wife gave me a warm welcome before accompanying me to the basement.

From the back of a small, soundproofed room, in which a magnificent hundred-year-old Bechstein stood resplendent, the Maestro's voice boomed:

'Welcome to the bunker!'

This somewhat unusual, rather amusing way of greeting me set the tone for the truly amazing jazz session – quite unlike any other I had ever known – that I was about to experience. The highlight of my afternoon was when Fabrice agreed to record some pieces with the two of us improvising together on the piano. Consequently, once this session in the presence of my pianistic hero was over, I was able to leave with a magnificent souvenir for posterity and, more importantly, proof that this surreal, dream-like experience had actually taken place!

✳

To round off the day in style, my husband and children had decided to prepare a special meal in my honour and were keen for me to return home as quickly as possible. With this in mind, I decided to take a taxi.

My decision turned out to be misguided; given the time of year, the city of Paris was just one massive traffic-jam. At one point, my taxi even ground to a complete standstill lasting a good twenty minutes.

Impatient to discover the fruits of my labour, I thus got out my little recording machine, plugged in my headphones and began to listen to the various improvisations I had performed with the Maestro.

Unfortunately, I could barely hear my music as it was being drowned out by the sound of the radio. I therefore asked the cabdriver if he would mind turning it off and allowing me to listen to my music without the headphones. Intrigued to discover that I had just emerged from a jazz session with a well-known pianist, he willingly obliged.

And so it was that, for the last ten minutes of my journey, the jazzy tones of my improvisations filled the car, producing, from what I could see, an increasingly large smile on the face of my young cabdriver.

Oh dear, I thought. *Is my music really that bad?*

When, finally, the car pulled up in front of our block of flats, to my great surprise the young cabdriver got out and walked all the way round to open the door for me. Next, he offered me his hand to shake mine! Then, he went one further in the surprise stakes by saying:

'*Madame*, thank you. Thank you so much for your mini-concert. For the last week, my clients have been talking about nothing else but Christmas. That is all I hear about, all day long, from morning till night. But you, well, by sharing your music, you have just treated me to the most wonderful, bluesy reprieve. And thanks to you, my day is ending on a complete high.'

Thanks to him the same could also be said for me!

THE PHILOSOPHER

As my telephone conversation drew to a close, I suddenly noticed a sign in the taxi indicating that the use of mobile phones was forbidden. Immediately, I offered my apologies to the cabdriver.

'I'm so sorry. I don't generally use my phone in taxis but this call happened to be really urgent so I had to take it.'

'No problem, *Madame*. I can make an exception for an urgent call. That said, since I was party to your conversation, I'd like to ask you a question. Are you a pianist?'

'Well... yes and no.'

The phone call had come from a piano hire service. Consequently, the cabdriver had heard me asking about the various types of piano available, the cost, whether it would be possible to book my personal piano tuner etc. – the reason for my enquiries being that I had recently been booked to play some piano jazz at a swanky Paris reception.

I pursued my reply to him with an explanation which, over time, has become fairly standard for me but which for some reason never fails to surprise the people to whom I give it.

'Initially, I trained as a translator. That is actually the reason I came to live in Paris. I arrived here straight out of university to pursue a career in translation, with a view to staying for two, maybe three years. But, after just one year, I met my husband – with the result that I never went back to live in England. As for the whole piano thing, well that came much later when I took a career break to raise our children.'

It was at this precise moment that I noticed my daughter, seated next to me, rolling her eyes to heaven in *the* most exaggerated manner before going on to whisper in my ear: 'T.M.I.'

Now, as anyone with children of her age will know, this is teenage speak for 'Too Much Information' which, in this particular case, could further be translated to mean: 'Mother, I'm begging you, please shut up. The cabdriver does NOT need to know your *entire* life story!'

Our darling daughter had indeed just embarked upon her teenage years, that most 'delicious' phase during which the vast majority of parents fall off their superhero pedestal with a brutal thud and metamorphose – in the eyes of their offspring – into weird creatures who, by dint of their very existence, are horribly embarrassing!

In spite of the 'T.M.I.' thing, I was under the distinct impression that the cabdriver was genuinely interested, especially as he then asked a question that has also, over time, become fairly standard:

'So, what sort of music do you like to play? Classical?'

'No. I play jazz.'

'Wow! What on earth made you want to take up jazz? Because, if you don't mind my saying so, it's really rare for a woman to play jazz.'

Well aware that I was about to provoke yet more eye-rolling from my daughter, out of politeness towards the cabdriver I nevertheless pursued the subject by explaining to him:

'Until very recently, I had a distinct feeling of frustration with music. As if I'd somehow missed the point. As a child, I loved the piano and clearly I had some ability because I used to play my favourite pieces by ear, long before I had even taken so much as a single lesson. Then, when finally I did start taking lessons at the age of nine, I progressed really quickly because I just loved it. However, after two years, for various reasons I had to give it up. My teacher retired and there weren't any other piano teachers in the small town where we lived. Also, with four children, my parents couldn't really afford extra-curricular activities. So after that, for many years, I continued by teaching myself. It was not until I reached my thirties that I was able to take piano lessons again. And when I did, I was delighted to discover that I still had the same ability in that every week I would easily learn to play whatever was thrown at me: Mozart, Chopin, Bach – you name it, I would learn it. On the other hand, classical piano no longer seemed to hold the same interest for me. You see, the thing is, once I could play these works, I would be at a loss as to what to do with them because I had absolutely no clue as to how to bring a personal touch to such great masterpieces. My feeling was, and still is, how could I – a mere mortal – possibly hope to add anything to works that for centuries have been immortalised as shining examples of musical perfection? To put it another way, taking up classical piano again made me realise that, in truth, I have a major failing when it comes to this type of music; the sad fact is I'm not actually very good at it at all because I simply do not know how to *interpret* the repertoire. All I can do is play the pieces. But my performance remains, at best, mechanical.'

'Well, put like that, I can understand that you were frustrated. But, then, what on earth made you take up jazz? How did you know that jazz would satisfy you when classical piano had left you feeling so very dissatisfied?'

'You know, it's a good question. I didn't know. I had no way of knowing. But most of the time it feels as if jazz almost came looking for me... One day, I received a surprise present from my father-in-law. It was a book of piano blues, in other words traditional jazz. I learned to play all the pieces really quickly and would play them almost obsessively. It was like a drug. And I was definitely hooked. Then, completely by chance, I met a piano teacher who specialised in jazz improvisation so I started taking lessons with him. Initially, I did it just for fun. After all, there was no pressure. It wasn't as if I had to produce a result. That said, before long, I realised that jazz was satisfying any frustration I may have had with music because I was, at last, discovering the freedom of expression that had eluded me for so very long. And, you know, the most amazing thing in all of this is that my progress was such that, after a mere few years of lessons, I actually began to play in public. Obviously, I would be quite incapable of performing solo on stage. I'll never reach that level. However, today, I am able to play background music in bars even though I never, ever expected to do this. It most definitely wasn't planned. Not for one single second did I think I would progress that far. But, then, life is full of surprises and music, it would seem, even more so.'

'Hence the hire of a grand piano? Is that for one of your performances?'

'Yes. It is.'

The cabdriver paused for an instant and then said:

'You know, *Madame*, I genuinely love this story of your road to jazz.'

'Is that so?'

'Yes. I do. I think it's wonderful that, when you were a little girl, life deprived you of piano lessons even though you had barely started them.'

'Really? What on earth could make you think that?'

'Clearly, this deprivation gave rise to a major feeling of frustration in you – musically speaking that is. Well, it's my opinion that this feeling was in fact most necessary for you to progress. You see it's precisely because of this that you continued to search – to dig deep – with a view to exploring other musical avenues. In other words, that which you perceived to be a source of frustration was in fact an indispensable guiding force, without which you may never have found your true musical calling. You know, it's a funny thing; often life will make the right decisions for us, even though we don't always realise it at the time. All we can do is work with what we've got. In your case, it really seems to have done the trick.'

27

While the cabdriver evidently did love the story of my long and winding road to jazz, for my part I genuinely loved his philosophical analysis of it.

Turned out I wasn't the only one.

My daughter also appeared to be listening attentively now. At least that was the impression she gave because, adding the ultimate icing to the cake that was this most interesting of conversations, she had – miracle of miracles – finally ceased to roll her eyes to heaven!

ANOTHER PHILOSOPHER...

That year, France was hosting the European Football Championship. As a result, all Parisian cabdrivers became obsessed with one thing, and one thing alone: the fan zone... and, more importantly, how to avoid it.

Now it so happens that I am perfectly ignorant in all matters relating to football because – my sincere apologies in advance to anyone who loves this sport for what I am about to say – the bottom line is football could not interest me less!

Be that as it may, one day I decided to make an effort because, within seconds of my getting into a taxi, the recurring theme of the fan zone was – yet again – raised.

Unfortunately however, since my heart wasn't really in it, it was somewhat absent-mindedly that I put the following question to the cabdriver:

'So, who are you for?'

I feared he might collapse from shock – not exactly my preferred response given his place at the wheel! – because it took him some time to get his breath back before he could reply:

'*La France! Évidemment!*'

In a bid to make up for my terrible *faux pas*, I endeavoured to pursue the subject by pretending that I knew something about it.

'Yes, yes of course. Naturally, you're for France. I'm sorry. I put the question badly. What I really meant was which French team do you usually support? Paris Saint-Germain?'

Even then, I only knew the name of this team because of my nephews! But, no matter, the cabdriver was now delighted not only to answer my question but also to justify his choice.

'You know, *Madame*, it's like this: I have lived in Paris for more than twenty-five years now but – I confess – I continue to support Marseilles. I know I shouldn't. But what can you do? I want to support a team I love. And the Marseilles team... well, there's nothing for it... I just love this team. With a passion...'

At this point, he paused for an instant as if – out of respect for the object of his 'passionate' love – he wished to observe a minute of silence.

Then he went on to say:

'*Mais oui!* That's love for you... Do we ever really have any choice? Do we actually choose the people we love? I don't think so. *Au contraire*, we have absolutely no control whatsoever over such matters. Take my case, for instance... My wife and I have been together for some twenty years now. And it is my hope that we shall be together for the rest of our lives. However, if one day she were to fall in love with someone else, it would be because she just couldn't help it. As for me, sadly there would be nothing I could do about it either, because that's the way it is. There's nothing you can do about it. All you can do is accept it. So, you see, I support the Marseilles team. And I accept it – even though I know I should support Paris Saint-Germain – because together, this team and I share a really beautiful, true love story.'

This time I chose to say nothing – content merely to smile – for my cabdriver's touching declaration had just reminded me of a particular aspect of life in my adoptive country that *never* ceases to amaze me: the astonishing ability of the entire French population to make an intellectual analysis of literally everything and anything. In other words, it is my humble opinion that only a Frenchman would be capable of taking a subject as down to earth as football (down to earth in every sense of the word, incidentally) and elevating it to the noble status of a philosophical reflection on the quite unpredictable nature of Cupid's work.

And by virtue of this most poetic take on a subject that, in the normal course of things, could not interest me less, my cabdriver had just scored one unbelievably fabulous cultural goal for France!

POK

Pok was a friend. And, being something of a wacko, a hugely entertaining one at that!

He acquired this nickname due to a simple error on my part: one day, I wrote him a text message while racing to get to an appointment and – as is always the way – only noticed my mistake after pressing 'send'. Consequently, I ended up writing a second message to explain:

'*Obviously, at the end I meant to write "OK" and not "POK".*'

He found this absolutely hilarious, deeming my mistake 'typical', because it is indeed my wont to be a tad impatient, always rushing to get things done as quickly as possible. And what really made him laugh is that I'd yet again fallen into that classic, counterproductive trap of, in my haste, ultimately taking more – not less – time to do something.

Suffice to say, this newfound word appealed to him so much that he began to use it, systematically, in all his messages.

'*Would you be free for lunch tomorrow? If so, just reply "POK".*'

Or...

'*Can I call you? I'd like to talk to you about something but, if you're not free, no worries. It's totally cool. POK?*'

Eventually, it got to the point where he was using the word so much that I actually ended up attributing it to him; from then on, he himself became Pok.

To my mind, this name suited him to a tee because it made me think of Puck, that mischievous, slightly rebellious, character in Shakespeare's *A Midsummer Night's Dream*. Indeed, while I was firmly convinced that my friend was a highly intelligent, exceptionally gifted man, he too – in the manner of his Shakespearean counterpart – had managed to retain a mischievous quality about him that rendered him both touching and, at times, incredibly funny. Naturally, in keeping with these qualities, Pok loved to make jokes about his newly acquired nickname. He would often say, for example, that his dream was to meet his Princess Pokette so that together they could have a whole bunch of *Poké-mômes*![4]

During the years I knew Pok, only once did I take a taxi with him. That said, I don't think I'll ever forget that particular cab ride, for it turned out to be – just like my wacky friend himself – something else!

*

That morning, Pok sent me a message asking on the off chance if I'd be free for lunch. When I replied with a – by now traditional – 'POK', he immediately wrote back:

'Brilliant. I have some absolutely bloody fantastic news to share with you!'

Pok had just landed the job of his dreams.

I was utterly thrilled. For weeks, I – together with a large group of friends – had been supporting him, encouraging him to aim as high as possible for, as is so often the case with highly intelligent people, in spite of his happy-go-lucky exterior, Pok was a deeply tormented man, riddled with self-doubt. Consequently, he felt a permanent need to be reassured about all his life-choices, be they professional or personal. And now that he had at last hit the professional jackpot, so to speak, he wished to express his thanks by inviting each and every one of us, one by one, to have lunch with him.

---

4   *Môme*: French slang for "child".

*

When I arrived at the restaurant, Pok could barely contain his excitement. The bottle of champagne he'd ordered stood a-cooling in a bucket on our table so naturally we began by raising a toast to his professional future. Then he asked me to help him write his letter of resignation – a gesture that typified the touching side to his character – so keen was he to share with me this momentous turning point in his life.

Once the letter was written, Pok's state of euphoria turned out – sadly – to be short-lived. Soon the profound anxiety, which characterised him and found its expression in a kind of pathological pessimism, began to take over.

'Oh no. What if it's the wrong decision?'

'What if I discover this job isn't so great after all?'

And so on and so forth…

In a bid to counterbalance his truly negative perception of that which in reality constituted *the* most superb professional achievement, I proceeded to go into raptures over the amazing future that lay before him.

Pok retaliated with:

'That's all very well but your comments actually say more about *you* than anything else. You know full well that you're just a big kid at heart, always going into raptures about absolutely everything and anything!'

He then went on to tease me with a joke that he loved to make about my personality.

'It would only take a fork for you to be ecstatic!'

With that, he grabbed one off the table and set about performing his usual hilarious imitation of me:

'Why thank you! Thank you so much. What a beautiful present! This fork is absolutely *amazing*. I do so love the colour of stainless steel… And have you seen how it comes equipped with four prongs? Oh, truly, I can't thank you enough…'

He would really make me laugh with his recurring joke. And while I'm not necessarily convinced that I am – as he would have it – the type of person who is capable of going into raptures about absolutely everything and anything (much as I would like to be), on the other hand I would regularly endeavour to explain to Pok that his life would be so much simpler if only he could avoid putting such a pessimistic spin on every single aspect of it.

I therefore undertook to defend myself regarding his performance with the fork:

'Hilarious! I'll grant you that. But, joking apart, while I agree that we live in a tough world, and at times a depressing one, I believe that you shouldn't only see the bad because our universe is also incredibly beautiful, don't you think? Let's just take one simple example. Whenever it snows, it's truly magical. And we all find it so utterly enchanting that we immediately turn into ecstatically happy little children. I bet even you do!'

'It's true. I love it when it snows.'

'But, you see, here's the thing... It's actually a million times more magical than the landscape simply turning white before our eyes.'

'Why's that?'

'Well, we should never forget – even though we do most of the time – that each snowflake is, in fact, a perfectly symmetrical six-point structure. Imagine, for one instant, the miracle of that: hundreds of thousands of perfectly symmetrical, tiny little works of art, each one different from the next, *all* falling from the sky at the same time. Now, don't you just find *that* truly magical?'

Pok was now wearing a familiar look that seemed to say: 'I rest my case; you're one big kid.'

*

With the lunch over, since Pok had an appointment in my neighbourhood, I suggested we share a taxi. Miraculously, in perfect illustration of our conversation in the restaurant, just as we got in the car it began to snow! And, immediately, we did indeed metamorphose into gleeful, overexcited children.

Especially me. With the result that, as the taxi turned into the *Place de la Concorde*, I could not help but exclaim:

'Just look at that! Isn't it absolutely fabulous!'

Teasing me once again, Pok pretended to revert to 'pessimistic mode'.

'I don't know... I really hate the big wheel they put up here. I think it totally spoils the view'.

But there was nothing Pok could do to dampen my enthusiasm.

'Well, let me tell you, for my part, it's not just that I *like* the big wheel. I truly *love* it. I go on it at least once a year. And it's genuinely worth it. You should do it one day. The view over the entire city is spectacular. On top of which, I don't know how anyone can think the big wheel is ugly. To me it's an incredible structure. It comes in the form of something akin to a rather large Meccano set. It's delivered in several truckloads at the end of November so it can be put up in time for Christmas. And it's amazing to watch as all those straight metal rods, together with several g-zillion nuts and bolts, somehow assemble into one beautiful, perfectly spherical structure. I just love it!'

Pok was now grinning at me with a look that seemed to say: 'How *do* you do it? How do you always manage to set me up with an opportunity to make a really obvious joke?' – before making *the* most pathetic joke of the entire day:

'Ah, I get it. What you're ultimately trying to tell me is that you just love a really good screw!'

Hmmm... And to think that, according to him, I was the big kid! It was a childish joke, of the type a hormonal teenager might be tempted to make to a girl he really fancies. Consequently, I started to roll my eyes to heaven, in the manner of a mother who is about to scold her child, before noticing that the cabdriver was also grinning from ear to ear and I too could not resist smiling.

My reaction incited Pok to tell a story that, this time, both the cabdriver and I found utterly hilarious.

Pok had recently organised a collection for a colleague who was about to retire. She was really looking forward to spending more time on her favourite hobby – doing DIY around the house – so Pok and his colleagues had clubbed together to buy the most enormous tool kit he had ever seen.

Upon opening her present, Pok's colleague had apparently exclaimed:

'That's great. Thank you all so much. At least now I can retire in style, happy in the knowledge that I'm guaranteed to get a really good screw!'

Better still, in response to the team's raucous laughter, she had insisted she was deadly serious adding:

'You may well laugh, but I mean it. Let's face it, it's not as if I'm going to get that from my husband at his age, am I?'

✶

Over time, with Pok's new job taking him to pastures new, we lost touch. So, sadly, I will never know whether Pok eventually managed to meet his Princess Pokette. Nor, indeed, if he finally overcame his innate pessimism in order to start appreciating the simple pleasures of life.

Be that as it may, of one thing I am quite certain. Never, *ever*, will I forget that cab ride which, I grant you, could seem a tad surprising at this stage of my narrative because, let's face it, our conversation in the car – however much it may have made us laugh – was anything but refined!

There remains, nonetheless, an important detail regarding this journey that I have yet to relate…

That day, I had the pleasure of witnessing *the* most unusual natural phenomenon. Generally, whenever it snows in Paris, the sky is white and the light a kind of austere grey. On this occasion, though, as the taxi turned into the *Place de la Concorde*, the sunlight was so utterly dazzling that the snowflakes, those hundreds of thousands of perfectly symmetrical tiny little works of art, each one different from the next, suddenly appeared to be adorned with mini rainbows, spontaneously transforming them into an exquisite shower of iridescent crystals. Never before – or since for that matter – had I seen anything quite like it; the sheer beauty of this spectacle, taking place before my very eyes, was almost unreal.

And it is precisely this magnificent, unusual, completely natural phenomenon that ended up turning my cab ride – which in the normal course of things would have been nothing out of the ordinary – into one superb, truly memorable, visual delight!

THE OPTIMIST

My journey, which should have taken around twenty minutes, was actually taking much longer. This was due to the massive traffic jams created by the large number of blue vans, out in full force across the entire city of Paris that night, ominously stamped with the words '*MISSION VIGIPIRATE*'[5].

Naturally, this incited the cabdriver and me to start discussing the recent shootings in France and the terrorist threat in general.

Then, after having spent a good half hour on the subject, the cabdriver – who had just pulled up at a red light – turned to me and said:

'I agree that, with all these attacks, we don't exactly feel safe. And ultimately, wherever we go in the world these days, danger never seems very far away. But you know, *Madame*, one day all of this will definitely stop.'

His tone of absolute certainty took me aback, causing me to stammer:

'Seriously…? Do you really think so?'

'Of course I do.'

'How can you be so sure?'

'Nothing, absolutely nothing, lasts forever in this world. So, it is perfectly logical to believe, one hundred per cent, that one day all of this will cease.'

Deluded idealism? Unreal optimism? Or just sheer madness?

---

5   *Mission Vigipirate* is the French anti-terrorist operation.

As I reflected on his most unexpected of observations, I could not help but think that my cabdriver did actually have a point. While his words were undoubtedly imbued with an almost childlike simplicity, on the other hand it was quite impossible to deny their veracity.

In fact, thinking about it, maybe it was *precisely* their childlike simplicity that made his words ring so very true. After all the proverb does say, does it not, 'out of the mouths of babes...'

My Very First Book and Nath

Publishing a book is tantamount to bringing a child into the world. Well, almost... Should this comparison appear a tad excessive, please bear with me while I explain.

Writing is one of *the* most amazing creative activities, one which the budding author initially keeps secret, preferring not to discuss it with anyone, for she (let's go with 'she' on this occasion given the comparison with childbirth) has absolutely no idea how it is going to pan out.

Then, as the weeks go by, timidly she'll begin to discuss it with those closest to her because they are beginning to observe a change in her; clearly she is no longer the same.

During the entire gestation process, the writer will give her creative project – an undertaking in which she firmly believes – her absolute all. In spite of this, she has no guarantee that it will actually come to fruition. And even if it does, she has very little control over the end product. Whatever she intended to write at the outset, in reality the creative process is in charge and it is better to treat that process with the greatest respect.

If all goes well, many months later – years even, in some cases – the fruit of several hundred hours work will be born: a beautiful literary baby.

To hold one's own published work for the first time is a highly charged, most emotional moment. And, from that point on, the author embarks on a different, equally gratifying phase: the book's promotion. It is at this stage that the work begins to take on a life of its own, writing a new story, its own

41

personal story, as it generates many surprising, unexpected, truly amazing experiences: positive feedback, press reviews, book signings and presentations that, in turn, give rise to wonderful encounters with people from all walks of life.

This is precisely how I experienced the publication of my very first book, *La jazz-girl passionnée et son dévoué accordeur*. In the manner of a proud first-time mother, the day I was finally, at long last, able to hold my own published work in my hands, I was absolutely ecstatic.

And, subsequently, the publication of my book did indeed lead me to have some truly magical experiences, one of which culminated in a cab ride quite like no other!

Here's what happened…

*

On that sunny winter's day, I was on a quest to find a piano tuner who works in a large piano showroom in Paris and who features in the fourth story of my book, titled in the English version: *The Piano Shop Showroom and a Most Surprising Surprise!*

(This is a story of a charming encounter. I go to a piano showroom to test two Steinways for a friend. A young piano tuner greets me and, since the place is empty, we start talking pianos – a subject about which we are equally passionate. Then as I go off to test the two designated instruments, the effect I inadvertently have is one of great surprise; after about half an hour, the young piano tuner comes back to offer me his personal thanks - together with those of his boss – for my performance, explaining how relieved they are not to have had the same old classical pieces inflicted upon them. According to him, it is extremely unusual – 'a breath of fresh air' – for pianists to play jazz in their shop. And, apparently, the ultimate in the unusual stakes is 'a woman who plays jazz'!)

I was so hoping to find this tuner because I thought – since he was in it – he might just like a signed copy of my book.

What I could not possibly know is that, by going on this quest, the very subject of my story – the 'my goodness you're a woman and you play jazz!' theme of surprise – was now about to repeat itself, punctuating various scenes of my existence, like some kind of running joke in an offbeat comedy!

*

I entered the shop and, on this occasion, was greeted by the manager:

'Good morning. How can I help you?'

'Hello. I've come in search of a piano tuner I met here, in this very shop, a few years ago.'

'Do you have a name?'

'No. I'm afraid I don't.'

With a slightly bemused look on his face, he replied:

'Well, you see, here's the thing. My entire sales team is made up of tuners. We have three shops and they rotate between them. So I'm sorry, but I really can't help you.'

Never one to give up easily, I decided to adopt another approach:

'I may not know his name. But I do know one thing about him.'

'Ah... and what would that be?' asked the manager, his bemusement now verging on irritation.

'The tuner's mother is German.'

Relief replaced his incipient irritation as he said:

'Now you're talking! That would be Étienne and he is currently working in one of our shops on the other side of Paris. May I ask why you want to see him?'

'Well, you see, I happen to be a jazz pianist and...'

He did not allow me to go any further. Suddenly, he had a really happy, excited look on his face. In fact, absolutely ecstatic would probably be a better way of putting it.

'You play jazz? You're a woman and you play jazz?? That's just soooo rare. Could you come this way, please?'

I followed him to the room at the end of the shop where, five years previously, I had tested the two Steinways. A client was playing a grand piano with a view to buying it. However – to my surprise and, I confess, great amusement – the 'wow, we have a female jazz pianist in our midst' factor seemed so much more important to the manager than a potentially lucrative sale, as he approached his client with the words:

'Could I just ask you to stop playing for a few minutes?' adding, as if this so obviously rendered his request totally legitimate: 'You see, a female jazz pianist has just come into the shop.'

The idea of ejecting this poor client from her seat was by now turning my amusement into embarrassment but, apparently unfazed by the request, she got up good-naturedly, enabling the manager to lead me to a concert Steinway, where he said:

'Would you mind playing something for me?'

A concert Steinway! Would I mind? I told him it would be an honour and a few minutes later, while I was playing, he sat down at the neighbouring piano and joined me in an impromptu jam session.

Once we'd finished, he exclaimed as if he still couldn't quite believe it:

'Wow! You really can play jazz. It's a sort of traditional, bluesy, New Orleans style, isn't it? I love it! But where does Étienne come in?'

I told him that I wanted to give a signed copy of my book to Étienne, explaining the reason why, and he suggested I come back the following Tuesday when Étienne would be there on desk duty. He also agreed to keep the book a surprise.

*

Four days later, I duly returned to the shop and this time the manager had the look of an excited child who had been asked to keep a secret but was literally bursting to tell it.

He greeted me with:

'Hello. I just can't wait to see Étienne's face when he discovers the reason you're here. He's working in the office in the basement. Follow me.'

Down the stairs we went to a small but exceedingly modern, hi-tech office. The manager walked in first and proudly announced:

'Étienne, this lady has come specially to see you.'

Étienne looked up and said, as if only a few days, and not five years, had elapsed since our first meeting:

'Oh, hello, I remember you. You're a jazz pianist, aren't you? What can I do for you?'

What a charmer, I thought. He can't possibly remember me after so long. Presuming that the manager must, after all, have let the cat out of the bag, I replied:

'You're kidding! The last time I was in this shop was over five years ago.'

Then, turning to the manager, I said: 'Surely, you must have told him why I was coming.'

The manager raised his hands in protest of his innocence, which Étienne proceeded to confirm:

'I can promise you that I really don't know why you've come to see me. But I do remember you coming here to test some pianos because you played jazz, for a whole morning, here in this very shop. You've no idea how rare it is to have a jazz player, let alone a female jazz player, come and test our pianos.'

The young Étienne was undoubtedly charming but, clearly, he was also genuine. He really did remember me. And, upon learning that he was actually the 'star' of one of the stories in my book, he was particularly touched to receive a signed copy.

*

As is often the case when I get talking to someone who is as passionate about pianos as I am, I had lost track of time and just left Étienne somewhat late for my next meeting. I thus jumped in a taxi and said:

'*Bonjour Monsieur*. I would like to go to the *Café de la Paix* on the *Place de l'Opéra*, please.'

'Off to have tea with our lady friends, are we?' was his surprising reply.

Hmmm... So no stereotypical assumptions there, then, I thought to myself, before saying:

'No. Actually, I'm going there to present my book... not to the entire café, you understand, but to a guitarist friend of mine.'

'Ah, so you're an author, are you?'

'Well, not exactly. I'm actually a translator by profession, but a few years ago I took up piano playing again. And then I wrote a book about it that I recently managed to get published.'

'Goodness. That sounds exciting. What sort of things do you play?'

'I'm a jazz pianist. But I'm not into anything dissonant and innovative. It's very traditional jazz...'

A slam on the brakes screeched the car to an emergency stop as the cabdriver turned round to look at me and say:

'Wow! That's just so unusual. You're a woman and you play jazz?'

Thinking to myself, there's nothing like a bit of mad Parisian driving to spice up the recurring question, I grinned at him and replied:

'As long as I'm still alive, I do.'

The surrounding cars were now tooting their horns, so he drove on and, smiling at me in the rear-view mirror, said:

'You have a slight accent. How long have you lived in Paris?'

'You're right. I'm not French. As you can hear, I'm English, but I've lived here for nearly thirty years.'

Referring to my 'as long as I'm still alive' comment, he asked:

'So still not used to Parisian drivers, then?'

'No,' I said resignedly. 'And I don't think I ever will become accustomed to them. It's the formative years and all that...'

'So, tell me about your book.'

Once I'd finished describing the main themes of my book – the birth of my passion for jazz improvisation, the fulfilment of a completely wild dream with the acquisition of my beautiful baby grand piano together with my discovery of the fascinating, mysterious piano tuning profession – the cabdriver said:

'You know, I really wish you every success with your literary venture. And I do believe you will succeed. When you talk about your experiences and your book, you have that joy, that happy enthusiasm, which all people who have a passion in life simply exude. And it's so contagious. Just talking to you has made me feel really happy, so much so that I would like to buy your book. In fact, I would like to buy two copies – one for me, and another for a friend of mine who plays the piano. Could you give me the title please, so I can order it?'

With a slam on the brakes, he screeched the car to a halt once again – this time in order to reach for a pen and paper. We were slap bang in the middle of the *Place de la Concorde!* The *Place de la Concorde!!* Help!!! I thought it probably best not to waste any time by saying that I actually had a pen and paper, as well as some business cards, on me. Instead, I just gave him the title in the hope that we could be on our way, without further ado, and that the increasing cacophony of tooting horns would consequently cease.

It was thus only a matter of seconds before the cabdriver started up his car again and, by dint of some miracle, actually managed to drop me off, safe and sound, at my chosen destination!

*

A few weeks later, I noticed that a certain Nath had given my book a serious thumbs-up by awarding it the maximum amount of gold stars, five out of five, and posting a lovely comment on my publisher's website.

It translates as follows:

'I have just finished reading this book and I loved it. The author has a true passion for pianos and jazz improvisation, a passion that radiates from every page, and she really knows how to convey that passion to the reader.'

As an author, it is naturally wonderful to receive such positive feedback; the undiluted pleasure I gain from writing every single word of my books, actually intensifies each time one of them is thus received.

And, with regard to this particular comment, I would just like to take the opportunity to extend my most sincere thanks to Nath because, while I have absolutely no idea who Nath is, I like to think it was the cabdriver.

THE CABDRIVERS IN BORDEAUX

That week we were in Bordeaux on what was quite the weirdest holiday we had ever been on.

My husband had just undergone a major operation. Given his relatively young age, he had been advised to put his life in the hands of a world-renowned specialist – a surgeon based in Bordeaux who was pioneering a highly innovative way of performing this surgery and achieving spectacular results.

We had planned this to coincide with the children's half-term holiday and, further to my husband's discharge from the hospital, had decided to stay on for a few days in case of any unexpected complications. Talk about convalescing in style. There we were, cocooned in the swanky surroundings of a four-star luxury hotel in the South of France!

During that strange week, because our hotel was slightly out of town, we were dependent on the local cabdrivers whenever we needed to go anywhere; to the chemist, the medical laboratory, the hospital appointments – and, indeed, for the occasional, more agreeable activity such as visiting the city of Bordeaux or, later in the week when my husband was feeling much better, the spectacular Saint-Émilion region.

I cannot remember any specific conversations with the cabdrivers in Bordeaux because, frankly, most of that week remains, to this day, a complete blur in my mind. That said, of one thing I am quite certain: I shall *never* forget the amazing kindness of the cabdrivers we encountered whenever they discovered the reason why we were holidaying in their town.

I decided to mention them here simply by way of a thank you.

THE SILENT TYPE

I got in the taxi and in response to my standard opening line – '*Bonjour Monsieur*, I would like to go to...' – the cabdriver remained perfectly silent, not even bothering to utter so much as a '*Bonjour Madame*', content merely to start the car.

It was like that for the entire journey; he did not utter a single word.

And even at the end of the journey he remained silent, pointing nonchalantly – indifferently even – to the amount displayed on the meter.

This caused me to ask him:

'Do you *ever* speak to your clients?'

'No.'

'Why not?'

'I don't see the point' was his most surprising reply, one so unexpected that I only just managed to refrain from bursting out laughing.

Conclusion: clearly this man had chosen completely the wrong profession!

THE COMPASSIONATE CABDRIVER

T hat day, it was my turn to be silent...
We were in the throes of an *annus horribilis*, a bleak
year during which a significant number of our friends
and relatives died. At one point, it got so bad that we found
ourselves going to a funeral once a week; the situation
was lugubrious to the point that it began to border on the
ridiculous – 'If it's Friday there must be a funeral' being the
joke of the moment. Naturally, by joking about this dire
situation, we were not being at all disrespectful. On the
contrary, our humour provided us with a very necessary self-
defence mechanism; it was our particular way of coping with
the terribly tragic events of the moment.

As far as I was concerned one of the hardest aspects
of those dark days was, as mother and pillar of the family,
having to remain strong for everyone. Our children were still
very young so it was of the utmost importance to be there
for them, to support them, to let them voice their fears and
sadness and to reassure them. And I have to say that we
were particularly proud of them during that year, as they too
stoically soldiered on, equally keen to maintain their sense of
humour, their own running joke being: 'Nobody is allowed to
spoil our vacation. If anyone dies during the school holiday,
we'll kill them!'

Be that as it may, their main survival strategy appeared to
lie in a fundamental need to reassure themselves that I was
actually okay – 'Don't be sad, Mummy' or 'Don't cry, Mummy,

please' – as if they were capable of dealing with anything life threw at them as long as their mother remained the same, unchanged, with a smile on her face at all times, whatever the circumstances. And, since that was all they apparently required to be able to carry on come what may, I was more than happy to do that for them.

It is, however, never good to repress negative feelings because, as we all know, this only seems to feed them allowing them to develop insidiously, thereby causing them to resurface at a later date with increased strength. So, even though I couldn't show my feelings in front of my children, it was extremely important for me to carve out moments of solitude in order that I too could let the barriers down.

Alone one morning, I was on the verge of succumbing to this very need when my husband invited me to have lunch with him. Holding back the tears once more, I accepted his invitation, telling myself that it would be better to get out and have a change of scenery, rather than stay at home weeping.

At the same time, doing this required huge levels of self-control; we ended up having lunch in a restaurant that was full of my husband's colleagues, with the result that I had to put on a show of normality, smiling and talking to them as if everything was absolutely fine.

It was a show that I was struggling to maintain by the time I got into a taxi to go home; I just about managed to stammer my address to the cabdriver but that was it.

Immediately, he turned off the radio – as if he had understood, without needing to be told, that I was desperate for some peace and quiet. During the entire journey, he maintained a respectful silence. And when, at last, he pulled up in front of the building where I live, he simply turned to me and said:

'*Madame*, do take care of yourself.'

Just like his silence up to that point, his simple words seemed to be worth all the compassion in the world. And somehow – I don't quite know how – he managed to say them in a tone of voice imbued with so much concern for my wellbeing, that I began to find it increasingly difficult to maintain my composure.

Thus it was that I swiftly alighted from the car – only just managing to utter a most grateful '*merci*' – and rushed up to our flat where, alone at last, I was finally able to open the floodgates and release the river of tears that had been seeking to flow from my eyes for so very long.

TALES ON SOME MOST UNEXPECTED COMPLIMENTS

As an antidote to the sad tone of the last three tales, I believe the time has come to recall a few cab rides on a really light-hearted (some would argue totally superficial and I'm inclined to agree!) subject.

Compliments. I just *love* receiving them. Let's face it, who doesn't? Especially when you're a girl, which is indeed my case!

I remember one day watching the French actress Emmanuelle Béart fire off a series of spontaneous answers to a questionnaire, during an interview with a well-known television presenter over here called Thierry Ardisson. Only one question momentarily floored her: 'Is there any type of compliment that you do not like receiving?' Here she had to pause for thought, before eventually declaring a resolute: 'No.'

I happen to agree with her. By that I mean I love receiving *any* type of compliment, even when I know full well that it is not sincere! To give you an example, whenever my son wants something from me he will start off with a little speech that, over time, has become our special ritual:

'Mummy, I really want you to know that I love you very much. You're the best mother in the world. And I would just like to add that you're looking particularly beautiful today.'

Obviously, his words are anything but sincere. I know this. My son knows this. What's more, he knows that I know that he knows! To put it another slightly less repetitive way, here we are playing our traditional game that precedes negotiation of any kind. And – I freely admit – I love this game for the delicious feeling of complicity it creates between us.

As a general rule of thumb, it is then fair to say that compliments make me smile, they brighten up my day, and this goes for all types.

Having said that, I also like receiving compliments because I can. By this I mean that, here in France, the cultural approach somehow makes it okay. And I fundamentally believe, as do other Brits who live in this country, that what makes it okay all comes down to the way feminism is perceived and defined in relation to the role of women in this society.

Please bear with me while I explain…

In England, back in my student days, I would regularly come across a certain category of feminist who appeared to take the concept of feminism to mean *equality* full stop, as opposed to *equality of rights*. The type of woman, who adhered to this mode of thinking, would react violently if a man dared to hold a door open for her, to offer to carry her heavy bag, or worse still if he had the audacity to pay her – shock horror – a compliment. Furthermore, this type of militant feminist, in order to send out a clear signal that she was equal to men on every level, would generally feel obliged to sport a most masculine look.

I remember, for example, one ardent feminist student friend of mine who would make a point of wearing the appropriate 'uniform' at all times. In other words, she dressed permanently in an old T-shirt and a pair of ripped dungarees – a 'style', if you can call it thus, she completed with a short, spiky haircut.

In France, as I see it, the approach is – if I may be so bold – more balanced because, over here, it is perfectly possible, positively encouraged even, to be - at one and the same time - *feminist* and *feminine*. The two are not seen as being mutually exclusive, which to my mind, is a very good thing. It so happens that my student friend from England also eventually came round to this idea when she spent a year in France as part of her studies. Upon her return, she looked really beautiful – a picture of femininity – having let her hair grow and having acquired a wardrobe full of chic little black dresses! Naturally, everybody teased her mercilessly about her surprising transformation. But she would unashamedly point out that the French way of life had taught her a more agreeable way to be faithful to her convictions; it was quite possible to be a 'girly' girl without in any way compromising her feminist principles.

It is because of this approach that people over here appear perfectly happy to accept, to celebrate almost, their clearly defined male or female status in society. And in this context, complimenting a woman is *not* tantamount to treating her as an inferior creature, or insulting her, far from it in fact.

Now before the militant feminist brigade lambasts me for expressing this potentially controversial, most politically incorrect (some may claim) opinion, allow me to be crystal clear: there is an obvious distinction to be made between a harmless compliment that makes a woman feel good about herself, which is acceptable in French society, and the type of remark that can make a woman feel ill at ease, which – as any normal person would agree – is totally unacceptable.

My best example of a harmless compliment that genuinely made me smile is the following: recently, a complete stranger, seeing me dressed in my dove-grey cashmere coat (worth every penny of the fortune it cost me, incidentally, because it regularly gives rise to some most unexpected compliments) declared to me in broad daylight, in a busy street, at the top of his voice:

'*Madame*, you really are very beautiful. Will you marry me?'

A militant feminist would most likely have slapped him across the face for his audacity. I, however, have lived in France for far too long to take offence at comments such as these so I replied:

'Sorry to disappoint you, *Monsieur*, but I'm already spoken for. Turns out I'm happily married. That said you never know what lies round the corner. So, thanks for the offer. I'll bear it in mind and keep you posted!'

The stranger burst out laughing, as did I, and then we each continued on our way.

He was neither a madman nor, from what I could see, a drug addict or an alcoholic, quite the contrary in fact. Here was an ordinary man who had just spontaneously made an out of the ordinary comment to an ordinary woman. This brief exchange made us both smile, brightening up what was otherwise a bleak winter's day. And I firmly believe that it would take a really warped personality to see any harm whatsoever in that.

It is with this in mind that I now share, on the following pages, some of the more memorable compliments I have received over the years from various Parisian cabdrivers. That is to say, I'm sharing them not because I believe I in any way deserved them – indeed, each time they took me by surprise – but because, in the context of a different cultural approach that I happen to like, it was okay to receive them. As my English friends over here would say: 'It could only happen in France.'

The other reason for sharing them is that I found these exchanges hugely entertaining; they brought a smile to my face and my hope is they will do the same for you.

An Omnipresent Fragrance

For as long as I can remember, I have worn the same perfume. From time to time, I think I should have a change, but my children won't allow it. As they see it, my perfume is my trademark.

On this particular occasion, it would appear that I might just have overdone it in the perfume stakes...

*

As I got into the lift in our block of flats, the deliveryman who was already there exclaimed:

'Wow! You smell nice.'

'Thanks', I replied, bursting out laughing, 'It's always reassuring to hear!'

'I love your perfume. It's...'

Then he totally amazed me by giving me not only the name of my perfume, but also that of the house that makes it.

'You're absolutely right. Well done!'

'There's no need to congratulate me, *Madame*. I know this perfume off by heart. My girlfriend wears the very same!'

*

Later that afternoon, as I rushed to make it to the school gates on time, I tried to overtake a woman who was walking a little too slowly for my liking. This turned out to be counterproductive because she actually slowed me down, stopping me to enquire about what now looked set to be the topic of the day.

'*Madame*, please believe me when I say that I don't usually stop complete strangers in the street to ask questions, but the thing is you just smell so nice! May I have the name of your perfume please?'

✳

Traditionally, the best is for last and this was no exception. By far the loveliest compliment I have ever received on my perfume came at the end of this surprising day, apparently dedicated to my omnipresent fragrance.

I got in the taxi and, before I could utter a single word, the cabdriver exclaimed:

'Wow! You smell amazing. *Madame*, with perfume like that you could charm the devil!'

A Persistent Accent

Although I left England over thirty years ago, my accent – it would seem – has never quite left me! Given that, as the chapter title suggests, this is the subject addressed here, this taxi tale only works if it's told in French. That is why I have chosen to leave it in the original version, with the translation underneath in italics.

✳

'Après le feu, c'est tout droit'
'At the traffic lights, it's straight ahead.'

'Vous pouvez répéter "tout droit" s'il vous plaît ?'
'Could you just repeat "straight ahead" please?'

'Pourquoi ? De toute évidence, vous m'avez déjà entendu…'
'Why? Clearly, you heard me the first time…'

'Ça, d'accord. Mais je voudrais vous réentendre. J'adore votre accent !'
'I'll grant you that. But I'd like to hear you again. I just love your accent!'

The Windswept Look

A strong wind was blowing over the city of Paris that day. Over my bobbed hairstyle too unfortunately – which struggles to be the sleek, sculpted creation that frames the face of Anna Wintour at the best of times! Consequently, during the cab ride, I spent a good while attempting to tame my hair back into some kind of shape. The thing is, I was about to spend another afternoon working on my jazz improvisations with my favourite pianist – Fabrice Eulry – and I had no wish to shock him by turning up looking more like an unkempt scarecrow than a music student!

Half an hour later the taxi pulled up in front of Fabrice's house, at which point the cabdriver turned to me and exclaimed:

'Wow! You didn't look anything like that when you got in the car. You look really beautiful now!' – *Thanks a bunch*, I thought! – 'What's changed? What's different about you? Did you put some makeup on?'

Warning to all men: DON'T ever say that to a woman. She will immediately think: *So, clearly, unless I'm wearing makeup I'm really ugly!*

'No, not at all, I already had my makeup on when I got in the car. I did, however, brush my hair. With the wind, it was all over the place.'

'Well, *Madame*, let me tell you, you look really beautiful like that!'

Talk about giving it to me straight! His direct comments made me burst out laughing, inciting him to add:

'You know, I'm paying you a genuine compliment here. Really, I am. You look amazing. When your hair is brushed properly, it completely transforms you.'

As I as struggled to hold back even more laughter in the face of his extremely personal comments, which he seemed more than keen to dish out under the guise of helpful advice, it was in a somewhat ironic tone of voice that I replied:

'Well, given the effect it's having, I'm happy to inform you that in future I shall be brushing my hair much more often!'

In spite of this, I could not deny that this cabdriver had just made me feel really good about myself. After all, if at my age all it took was well-brushed hair for me to look – as far as he was concerned – 'amazing', then I couldn't exactly complain, could I? In other words my little ego was feeling tremendously flattered by his unexpected comments!

Naturally, I was about to be suitably punished for this brief moment of self-satisfaction. Naturally in every sense of the word since it was only a matter of time before the elements put me firmly back in my place...

As I alighted from the car, *the* most enormous gust of wind immediately sent me back to square one. Thus it was that, in spite of my best efforts, I did indeed arrive at Fabrice's home looking more like a dishevelled scarecrow! Quite unlike the genius of a pianist – known to those in the profession as the Chopin of boogie-woogie – who was now standing before me and who, with his customary sartorial elegance, had donned a stylish trilby hat to come and meet me at his garden gate.

Be that as it may, I could no longer feel remotely bothered about what my hair looked like, for presently there lay before me an afternoon entirely dedicated to my great passion in life... jazz!

THE EYES OF A FILM STAR

A s if to proclaim loud and clear that spring was on its way, the sun was out in full force. Consequently, people appeared to be in a really good mood, the dazzling Parisian sunlight having had the magical effect of putting a smile on everybody's face.

The power of this magnificent weather, heralding the end of winter, to transform the overall mood was particularly evident in the case of my cabdriver that day. Here it would be fair to say that this young man was not simply joyful; he was positively overexcited!

Thus it was that, as I got into the taxi - before I could even utter a single word - he exclaimed:

'Oh my God! Wow! I just *don't* believe it… *You* have exactly the same eyes as my girlfriend!'

Surprised and somewhat taken aback by this most original way of greeting a client, initially I was at a loss for words.

Be that as it may, as I sized up this drop-dead gorgeous, Hollywood film star of a cabdriver, I could only assume that his girlfriend was, in all likelihood, young and extremely beautiful too. And that is why, by way of a reply, I offered a tentative 'Err… thank you?' spoken in a tone that was both questioning – since I had no guarantee that my assumption was right – and sceptical, because the idea that I could possibly resemble the sort of girl he would be with, even in the tiniest of ways, stuck me as being a tad far-fetched!

The young cabdriver therefore deemed it necessary to clarify his assertion by adding:

'I can assure you it's true. You have exactly the same eyes as my girlfriend! And yes, it is indeed a compliment. You know, my girlfriend really is very beautiful.'

Of that, I most definitely did *not* require any convincing!

My charming young cabdriver was, however, determined to prove his point; at the next red light, he produced a telephone with quite the largest screen I had ever seen, one that was now filled with a picture of his significant other's face.

As I had imagined, his girlfriend was – just like him – breathtakingly beautiful. The spitting image of Penelope Cruz, in fact, which is why I could not help but burst out laughing because any possible comparison between this beauty and me now appeared completely absurd. Perhaps, at this point, it would be useful to point out that I have a diaphanous complexion, pale green eyes and that my short, bobbed hair is naturally ash-blond. In other words, the physical differences between the two of us could not have been more enormous!

Appearing slightly offended, the young cabdriver asked me:

'Why are you laughing? Don't you think she's beautiful?'

'But of course I do. No question. She looks absolutely amazing. It's the comparison that's making me laugh. It's extremely flattering. And I truly thank you for your compliment because if you can see any resemblance whatsoever between your beautiful girlfriend and me – however small it may be – then, believe you me, that makes me very happy. That said, I have to admit, I can't see any similarity at all, and that goes for our eyes too.

Now reassured as to my opinion regarding his girlfriend's looks, my charming young cabdriver recovered his initial exuberance to conclude on the subject with a final flourish:

'I promise you, I'm not kidding; you really do have the same eyes. I could not possibly be mistaken about this colour. It's so rare to see such clear green eyes; I never grow tired of looking at them. And you know what? I can't wait to see my girlfriend tonight so I can tell her that today I dropped off a client with exactly the same unusual eyes!'

At this point, I deemed it wise to keep my mouth firmly shut. While I was quite convinced that this type of remark would not go down at all well with his girlfriend, on the other hand I was not about to explain why. Doing so would have required me to address the vast, extremely complex subject of the sensitive female psyche. And I had no wish whatsoever to dampen the enthusiasm of this charming young man whose unexpected, touching, spontaneous comments had just put one huge smile on my face, far bigger than that bestowed upon me by the beautiful weather, and one that was to remain there for the entire day!

Eyes to Remember and the Sweet Offer of... a Sweet!

B reaking the silence of the first ten minutes of my journey, the cabdriver put a question to me:

'Would you like a sweet?'

'No thank you.'

'Are you sure?'

'Yes. Quite sure, thank you.'

'The sweets come free, you know. They're on the house!'

His insistence made me laugh and caused me to give a slightly more detailed answer:

'It's very kind of you but, the thing is, I don't like sweet things. So you see, it really is a "no", a completely sincere "no".'

I was also laughing for another reason. Two weeks previously, I had taken this very same taxi. I knew this because I had had exactly the same conversation with this man, word for word. I had therefore already met this charming, sweet-dispensing cabdriver and was highly amused by this situation that was seeing me take the same taxi, for the second time, in a fortnight.

The most amusing part, however, was still to come...

At the end of the journey, the cabdriver turned round and exclaimed:

'Well, well, well! I know you, don't I? You've taken my taxi before. About two weeks ago, if I remember rightly.'

'You're right. I remember you very well because it's most unusual to offer sweets to a client. On the other hand, I'm really surprised you remember me. As a cabdriver you must come across so many people, even over the relatively short space of time of a fortnight.'

'Indeed I do. But only very rarely do I come across eyes like yours. It's because of your eyes *Madame*. How could I possibly forget such eyes!'

Clearly, I thought, *my eyes are something of a hit with Parisian cabdrivers!*

As I stepped out of the taxi, this unlikely situation incited me to say:

'So, see you in two weeks' time then!'

'What do you mean?'

'Generally, things come in threes don't they? So, logically, I shall see you again, in two weeks.'

'Well, *Madame*, if it happens a third time, you do realise we'll have to celebrate it; next time I'll take you out for a drink!'

His offer to go out for a drink was not threatening in any way. On the contrary, it was made in the very spirit of harmless banter that I too had used. And that is exactly how I took it.

Unfortunately, the same cannot be said of the invitation in the tale that follows…

THE CREEP

I was in the process of putting my purse away when the cabdriver said:

'I've just come to the end of my shift. Would you like to go for a drink with me?'

'No, thank you.'

'Oh, I see, you're not free this evening. Well, never mind. Here's my card. Call me when you are free and we'll meet up for a drink.'

My response to his audacious comments – spoken in a direct tone that I really didn't appreciate – was a very firm 'NO', to which he said:

'What? Don't you want to go out with me?'

His persistence threw me completely off balance and, although I was under no obligation whatsoever to give him an answer, stupidly I began to do just that as if, somehow, I had to justify myself:

'No, I don't want to go out with you. Not with you, or with anyone else for that matter. I happen to be very happily married.'

His tone was now contemptuous as he pursued the subject with:

'And does this mean you're not allowed to go out? Can't you even have a drink with someone? Is your husband the type of bloke who doesn't give you any freedom, or what?'

By now, I was beside myself with rage; with lightning speed, I got out of the car and slammed the door behind me.

Unfortunately, I could still sense that this creepy man was watching my every move as I walked swiftly to the main door of our block of flats. So I hid my hand, while typing in the security code to prevent him from seeing it, entered the building and got straight in the lift that was, thankfully, already on the ground floor.

Once safely home, I was so shaken by what had just happened that I immediately told my husband all about it, concluding with this sad thought:

'I just don't believe it. To think that, at my age, somebody has just tried to pick me up. You would have thought that the one advantage for us females of growing old would be that at least we'd get less harassed, less bothered by seedy men.'

It was at this point that my husband took it upon himself to defuse the situation with that most effective, time-honoured remedy that is humour. Adopting an air of exaggerated pride and speaking in an undeniably macho tone, he replied:

'But of course people are always going to want to pick you up, *ma chérie*. What happened doesn't surprise me in the least. After all, we're not just talking about any old woman. We're talking about MY wife. My very own, beautiful wife!'

His comments were quite ridiculous. All of a sudden, for very different reasons, the cabdriver's behaviour seemed equally ridiculous. And in the end, I too could see that the best thing to do, the only thing to do in fact, was have a good laugh about it!

The Wacko

I t was late when we left the dentist. On top of which, it was extremely cold. So we were delighted when we spotted a cab rank just outside the practice.

As we got into the first cab in the queue, I was surprised to see that the cabdriver was watching a small television. Even more so when he started the car without bothering to turn it off!

I therefore did not deem it unreasonable to request:

'*Monsieur*, could I just ask you to turn off your television please?'

'Why?'

'Because, surely, you're not going to drive and watch the television at the same time?'

'Oh yes, I am. Don't worry, *Madame*, I'm quite used to doing it. I do it all the time.'

'Well, *Monsieur*, allow me to make myself very clear: there is absolutely no way that you are going to drive my two children and me while you watch television. So could I kindly ask you to stop the car please?'

Without saying a word he did as I asked, whereupon we leapt out – delighted to have got away – and approached the second cab of the rank.

*

Clearly it was going to be one of *those* evenings because the cabdriver of the second cab greeted us with:

'Sorry, but I'm not going to take you.'

'Why is that?'

'It's out of respect for my colleague, *Madame*. You simply cannot jump the queue, you have to go with the order of the rank.'

'Well, I can see your point. But the thing is your colleague wants to watch his television while he drives. To me this is unacceptable. In fact, it's extremely dangerous.'

'Now you listen here, *Madame*. This is so not my problem. All I know is that I'm not going to take you. Clearly, you are one difficult client. And I can quite do without clients like you!'

*

Third time lucky, we got in the next cab of the rank where I started by explaining to the cabdriver precisely why we had no choice but to do so, concluding with:

'I just don't get it. Asking a cabdriver to turn his television off seems like a perfectly reasonable request to me. But apparently this makes me a difficult client.'

'Okay, I'll take you. But you must understand that I'm making an exception here. I don't normally do this to my colleagues.'

In spite of his reservations, I presumed the difficult part was now behind us.

Naturally, I hadn't banked on how this cabdriver would react upon hearing the address of my destination:

'Are you *sure*?'

Going home in a taxi was turning out to be extremely complicated; his question threw me completely off balance, causing me to stammer:

'Err… yes. After all, that's where I live… so I don't think there's too much chance of getting it wrong.'

'I'll grant you that. But I prefer to check because you're a woman. And you women, well frankly – let's face it – you're *always* changing your minds!'

By now I was at the end of my tether with the cabdrivers of this rank and sorely tempted to slap him across the face for his sexist comments.

My children also looked utterly horrified. So much so that I was about to give up on the idea of going home in a taxi when, suddenly, something made me think twice about how I should respond...

Evidently, this was no ordinary cabdriver; on the contrary, he came across as a bit of a wacko who, into the bargain, couldn't give a toss about political correctness. And, I freely admit, I too can get really fed up with the politically correct brigade on occasions.

Consequently, instead of slapping him, I chose to reply:

'Well, *Monsieur*, I'm delighted to confirm that I have just given you the correct address... and also that I am in complete agreement with your view of the female species.'

I then went on to explain the reason for my acquiescence:

'You've no idea. The number of times I'll tell my husband "No, I don't want any coffee", when he makes it at the weekend. And you know what, he'll still make me one, justifying it by saying: "I know you told me you didn't want any, but I was convinced you'd change your mind so I thought I'd make you one anyway." And, I have to admit, nine times out of ten, he's right!'

'Well there you go. I told you I had a point. And do you know how I know this? The fact of the matter is, *you* have no idea of the number of times female clients will give me an address and then, during the journey, they'll see something in a shop window – a dress, or a pair of shoes – and they'll say: "*Monsieur*, stop the car please. Now! I've changed my mind and I have to get out right here." *Eh oui!* That's just how you women are.'

He really made me laugh with his 'no holds barred' comments, causing me to say:

'Well, in theory, the address I've given you is the right one. But, since I'm a woman, we're just going to have to wait and see, aren't we? I can't promise you anything...'

After this slightly unorthodox start, for the rest of the journey – contrary to my initial expectations – I had a really pleasant time talking to this cabdriver whose apparent goal, when on duty, was to transform potentially mundane cab rides into entertaining mini-slices of life!

And when at last we did arrive in front of our building, I couldn't help but tease him back by pretending to challenge him with:

'Turns out, *Monsieur*, you're wrong about us women. Let's face it, you cannot deny the fact that I gave you one very specific address at the beginning of this journey and just look how I've managed to stick to it, all the way home.'

But there was nothing for it. Snorting with laughter, he retorted:

'But that actually makes complete sense. You see, *Madame*, there's always the exception that proves the rule!'

ANOTHER WACKO!

I grew up round here and I've never seen anything quite like it! Do you realise that on the 25th December the weather wasn't just mild. It was really hot, twenty-five degrees! Talk about a great Christmas present! I do hope you're going to be able to get a bit of skiing in. But, frankly, it's not looking good. They've only managed to open three slopes. You have to take a bus to get there. And, even then, it's artificial snow...'

We had just arrived in the Alps for our winter holiday. And, that particular winter, the weather was indeed exceptionally mild. To add insult to injury, there was no way our female cabdriver was going to let us forget it because she was on a roll that saw her determined to talk about it non-stop.

'You know it's really hard to greet people here. They get off the train, and – already – they're disappointed. Disappointed at the beginning of a holiday... it's just not right.'

She didn't seem to understand that her doom and gloom speech was actually making matters much worse! With or without snow, we were determined to enjoy our week in the Alps and we really could have done without her depressing comments.

Sadly, though, there was to be no reprieve as she went on to address every last aspect of the unfavourable weather conditions, informing us for example of the effect this would have on the local economy – 'We're all going to have a terrible season' – before moving on to the cause of the problem at a worldwide level – 'This is all down to global-warming, you know' – as if she were revealing some kind of scoop, a hitherto little-known item of breaking news!

Then, just when we thought the picture could not get any gloomier, she actually managed to up the ante by suggesting a solution to the problem that was even *more* unorthodox than her way of greeting her clients:

'You know, if this continues, I think I'll just meet people at the station with a gun. That way, upon their arrival, they can immediately put a bullet through their head and be done with it, once and for all!'

In the back of the car, we were in fact already 'killing' ourselves ... laughing!

While our 'charming' cabdriver's chosen profession undoubtedly required her to cover some distance on a daily basis, on the other hand, when it came to tourist relations, clearly she still had quite some distance to cover!

THE CONSIDERATE CABDRIVER

T hat night I was trying to get my young daughter to the doctor, fast. As a child she rarely got sick, but when she did she didn't do things by halves. And, on this particular occasion, there was something major going on with her lungs.

Our cabdriver, who hailed from Morocco, seeing that his little passenger was unwell, began the journey by asking me about the precise nature of the problem. Then, he took it upon himself to come up with a diagnosis. Finally, he advised me as to how I should treat the affliction!

He was convinced it was pneumonia and suggested we have recourse to his grandmother's tried and tested remedy, one by which his entire family swore.

It turned out that our cabdriver's grandmother, who still lived in Morocco, had for many years enjoyed a hugely successful career as a professional opera singer – this in spite of her fragile health leaving her prone to frequent lung infections – because she had a secret weapon, a magical cure. It came in the form of a weird, disgusting potion. (Disgusting, that is, according to the face my daughter pulled when she heard the description of it and I have to say I couldn't help but agree with her.) Concocting the potion was simple; serious quantities of honey and olive oil would be blended together. And, so convinced was his grandmother of the miraculous powers of this somewhat dubious liquid, that in later years she continued to swear by this – and this alone – when it came to treating the children, grandchildren and great grandchildren of her family, whatever the ailment, whenever they were ill! Consequently, according to our cabdriver, nobody in his family had ever taken a single antibiotic!

Encouraging us to adopt his family's panacea, the cabdriver gave me the precise recipe and begged me to try it for 'just one night', concluding his would-be doctor speech with:

'Please try it *Madame*. After all, you've nothing to lose.' – *Only my daughter!* I thought, slightly horrified – 'If it doesn't work, you can give your daughter her *prescribed* medicine tomorrow.' At this point he used a decidedly derogatory tone, practically spitting out the word prescribed, in order to express his disgust at the idea of opting for a more standard type of treatment. 'But I'm quite sure you won't need it. In fact, I'm so sure that I'm going to give you my telephone number. That way, you can let me know exactly how your little patient reacts to our way of treating infections. Call me tomorrow morning. I'm convinced you'll ring me to say she's completely cured!'

Out of politeness, I took his card.

*

Once we got to the doctor, she confirmed what we had all feared (including the cabdriver, as it happened): it was indeed pneumonia. And, since my daughter was already decidedly weak, drastic action was required. In other words a course of heavy-duty antibiotics was quite simply unavoidable.

Obviously, it was my firm intention to follow the doctor's orders to the letter. There was no way that I was going to take the slightest risk with my little princess by experimenting with an antiquated remedy – one that naturally caused the doctor to fall about laughing when I related my conversation with the cabdriver to her!

*

A few days later, thanks indeed to the prescribed course of antibiotics, my little patient was a lot better. And all I could think was how lucky we are to live in a country where this kind of treatment constitutes the norm.

At the same time, so convinced was our cabdriver of the success rate of his recommended 'medicine' that I do sometimes wonder what would have happened had I actually dared to test his weird cocktail of honey and olive oil ...

THE CONSIDERATE DAD

It was the night of *the* annual dance show and my son and I were running incredibly late. Worse still, it was the one year when it was extremely important for us to get there on time because my daughter was already terribly disappointed that my better half, i.e. her father, couldn't make it due to a business trip in the States.

Given the time of day, we decided the quickest way to go there would be by public transport. But that night, as luck would have it, due to a technical problem our *métro* line was quite suddenly closed down.

Emerging from the *métro* station back into the street, we were thus extremely relieved to spot a taxi approaching. Sadly, though, our relief was to be short-lived because barely had I announced the address of our destination when the cabdriver replied:

'I'm sorry, *Madame*. I've just finished for the day and my wife and children are in a hurry for me to get home. Had you been going somewhere that was on my way, I would happily have taken you. But sadly it's not the case. I'm going in completely the opposite direction!'

'Oh no, that's all we needed!' I exclaimed, before going on to apologise. 'I'm so sorry. This is not your problem. I totally understand that you're in a hurry to get home. It's simply that we're trying to get to my daughter's dance show and we're already really late. But, like I said, it's not your problem. *Au revoir, Monsieur.*'

The cabdriver thanked me for my understanding, started the car, and continued on his way.

He had only driven a few yards, however, when he stopped and gestured for us to approach him, whereupon he said:

'Go on get in. I'll take you. I know how disappointed my own daughter would be if I were to arrive late for one of her shows.'

His kindness was duly rewarded.

Miraculously, for a Saturday evening in Paris, there were no traffic jams. Consequently, just ten minutes later, the cabdriver dropped us off right in front of the main entrance of the *Théâtre de Neuilly*.

Against all logical expectations, we thus arrived somewhat early for the show!

As for the considerate family man who had driven us there, given the surprising lack of traffic that night, he still looked set to make it home on time.

All's well that ends well!

THE
CONSIDERATE PASSENGER

On that cold winter's night, as the family gathering drew to a close, my husband offered to drive his parents home. Naturally our children wanted to go too, which meant there wasn't enough space in the car for me.

Thus it was that I found myself taking a taxi to go home, on my own.

*

Barely had I arrived in our flat when my husband called me from the car, on our landline, to announce somewhat enigmatically:

'You don't have your mobile phone with you.'

'I don't understand. What do you mean?'

'*You* no longer have your mobile phone with you.'

'What on earth are you talking about? Why do you keep mentioning my mobile phone?'

'Take a look in your handbag.'

He was right. My phone was nowhere to be seen – and with good reason as it happened. I had apparently left it behind on the seat of the taxi!

Thankfully, the next passenger had found it and had had the good sense to call the last person I'd called who just happened to be my husband.

Better still, it turned out that this young man was a waiter in a local restaurant, really near where we live, and he had obligingly told my husband that I could drop by in the morning to retrieve my lost object.

*

The next day, seeing that I was busy, my husband offered to go and pick the phone up on my behalf – an offer I duly accepted – and just as he was leaving, I handed him an envelope containing a bit of money to give to the waiter as a token of my gratitude.

Poor guy. When I think how kind and considerate he'd been. Yet, in addition to my small financial reward, he was about to receive a major 'punishment' for his altruistic act.

Imagine, for one instant, the merciless teasing that ensued when my husband entered the restaurant and said to the young waiter, at the top of his voice, for all to hear:

'Hello. I believe you have my wife's mobile phone.'

ANOTHER
CONSIDERATE CABDRIVER!

S pring was upon us and the delightful prospect of a four-day bank holiday weekend was fast approaching. As we weighed up our options as to how to spend it, with our son away at school in the UK, my husband finally decided to spit it out and tell us what he really wanted. Deep down, he was hankering after a few days in Normandy where he would be able to do some really hard-core sailing with a bunch of like-minded friends. In order to render his maritime plans acceptable he had – credit where it's due – a most appealing suggestion to make to my daughter and me, an offer we couldn't refuse that came in the form of an all-expenses paid trip to Italy! Frankly, we didn't require much convincing. It took us mere nanoseconds to select a swanky hotel in the sumptuous setting of Lake Maggiore.

*

On the morning of our departure, as we announced our destination – Charles de Gaulle airport – the cabdriver said:

'So, we're off on a girls' trip are we?'

'Absolutely!'

'Okay, let's go through the list. Do you have your passports with you?'

'Yes.'

'Your mobile phones?'

'Yes.'

'Your money?'

'Yes.'

'Have you locked your front door? *Madame*, do you have your keys with you?'

'Yes.'

'Well then, we're good to go aren't we? You can now set off without a care in the world!'

Not for the first time, I found myself thinking: This could only happen in France.

Our jovial, upbeat cabdriver really made us laugh with his fun checklist and, thanks to him, from the moment we got in the cab we were already in a great holiday mood!

The Business Lawyer

(Also, as it turned out, an extremely considerate man.)

With a view to ending on a high note – at least I hope so (!) – to conclude, I have chosen this tale, one of my absolute favourites.
It doesn't take place in a taxi itself, but rather in a queue at a cab rank. Be that as it may, I decided to include it here because the exchange that follows touched me to such an extent that I have *never* forgotten it.

✶

It was the beginning of August.

Barring tourists, Paris tends to be a rather empty city during this particular month so I was surprised to see a long queue as I approached the cab rank.

It didn't really matter though. I was in no particular hurry. The weather was gorgeous and I was happy to be outside.

A few minutes later, several taxis arrived all at the same time with the result that, suddenly, there was only one person left waiting in front of me: a handsome, forty-something man elegantly dressed in a black suit, a crisp white shirt and a pink silk tie.

✶

For a good while now, the forty-something man had been nervously alternating his eyes between the long avenue stretching out before us, where he was clearly hoping to spot a taxi, and me.

Then, finally, letting out a large sigh while at the same time alluding to my huge balloon of a stomach, he said:

'*Madame* I know I really should let you go first, but the thing is I'm extremely late for my meeting.'

I was indeed heavily pregnant. 'About to pop' as they say. And I had just left a bookshop clutching a bag full of newly purchased books, for I was harbouring the ridiculous notion that I would actually have time to read (!) during my five day stay in the maternity clinic.

I happen to like reading books in French just as much as in English. That day, however, I had chosen to go to one of Paris' few English bookshops with a particular purchase in mind: Adam Gopnik's *Paris to the Moon*. Although I had read this book many years previously, I could no longer lay my hands on my copy of it and I really wanted to read it again. More specifically, I wanted to find the passage explaining the meaning of the expression '*le choix du roi*' because I myself was about to make the 'king' very happy indeed. Yes, you've guessed it, as the proud mother of a lovely little boy I was now preparing to welcome a baby girl into the world!

In order to put the anxious man currently standing before me at ease, I replied:

'Don't worry. It's really not a problem. I'm happy to be outside, in the sun.'

Relief appeared to wash over him as he explained:

'Thank you so much, I appreciate it. You see, the thing is… well, I can't really expect you to understand but… I happen to be a business lawyer and I'm very late for my meeting. And, the fact of the matter is, this meeting is *absolutely* crucial for my career.'

Flashing him a wide smile, I replied:

'On the contrary, I quite understand. My husband is a business lawyer too. I know how it is.'

A few minutes later, the lawyer let out another deep sigh and then said:

'I'm sorry, but I can't do it. I just *can't* do this to you. Even if *you* don't mind waiting, *I* have no choice but to give up my place.'

'You know, I really do mean it when I say it's absolutely, totally *not* a problem. I was under strict orders to spend a large part of this pregnancy resting. You've no idea how delighted I am to be standing up at long last.'

'It's very kind of you to say so. But, you see, it's also out of respect for my wife and children.'

In a touching tone of voice, he went on to explain:

'I wouldn't want someone to do this to my wife. I expect people to treat her decently; the same goes for my children. And, in light of that, the least I can do is treat other people decently. So I *must* give up my place. I simply don't have the choice.'

This sensitive man's desire to do the right thing by me and, by extension, his family left me feeling extremely moved and keen to reassure him further:

'I do appreciate your considerate words, truly I do. But please understand that when I say I'm delighted to be standing up, I mean it. Believe you me, enforced rest is not easy but it has all been worth it. Apparently everything is looking good now. And, as I'm practically at full-term, the doctor has said I can do anything I want... Well, apart from bungee jumping that is!'

My attempt to defuse the situation with humour did little to convince him, so I decided to adopt another tactic.

'Maybe we could share the next cab that arrives? That way, you'll be reassured to see me sitting down *and* you'll avoid any further delay. Where are you going?'

'Bercy.'

As luck would have it, his destination was at the complete opposite end of Paris to mine. And when I told him that, the poor guy looked more frustrated than ever.

In order to reassure this most considerate man, once and for all, I would have loved to be able to explain to him much more precisely why, on the contrary, I really, truly, wanted to wait; the mere act of standing up – a simple undertaking for others – was, in my case, proof that a seemingly endless personal struggle was at long last, *finally*, coming to an end. Consequently, I was actually savouring this banal act as if it were some kind of rare, exotic pleasure!

But how an earth could I possibly make him understand that? To do so, I would have had to turn back the clock, a very long way indeed ...

*

I once heard an expression in a film that goes something like this: 'If you want to give God a good laugh, tell him about your future plans.'

On that basis, when we got married, I think the good Lord quite probably had tears of laughter streaming down his face!

As young newlyweds we had a plan: our dream was to have three or four children, very close together. And I felt particularly lucky in that my husband already loved babies – something some of my female friends really envied – so much so that he didn't take any convincing about making the leap into parenthood.

Naturally, we could not possibly know that it would take us four difficult years, riddled with major complications, to bring our first child into the world.

I simply do not have the words to describe the depths of our despair during that period. All I can say is this: never before had we felt so alone and isolated. Throughout those long drawn-out years, we lived as if in some kind of exile, publicly sharing the joy of all those around us – as they successfully started their families – while privately weeping our tears of grief.

To make matters worse, as if our despair were not already bad enough, we also found ourselves having to put up with an absolute ocean of tactless comments. There were those who regularly granted themselves the luxury of complaining about their parental status, so very envied by us: 'I've just had a terrible weekend. I didn't sleep a wink. Our son has an ear infection!' Then there were those who had the temerity to suggest that the problem was purely psychological (this despite the fact that during those years I had to undergo several operations to correct various clinically identified physical problems) and, therefore, my fault: 'Don't go getting obsessed about it, now. If you think about it too much, you'll never have a baby!' And finally, the worst ones, the show-offs: 'You know this has never been my problem. Me, well… I only have to look at my husband and I'm pregnant!' Understandably, I found comments such as these particularly hard to hear.

In short, prior to those desperate years I did not know that such tactlessness was actually possible. At the same time, these reactions taught me that we were experiencing a quite particular kind of grief, of an atypical, misunderstood nature. The couple that struggles to have a child constantly carries within them an intense feeling of loss. Permanently, they miss someone. Yet that someone is a person they have never actually known. How could anyone possibly understand that if they haven't experienced it themselves? The vast majority of people are able to understand that to lose a close friend or family member causes intense grief. But the fact that such grief can be felt for the *absence* of a person who has never even existed, remains a notion that is quite simply incomprehensible to that very same majority.

And if today, twenty years later, I have finally mustered up the courage to write, here, about this particular form of suffering, it is because (in addition to this being, as I said, one of my favourite taxi tales) my hope is that by sharing my story I might just help other people, currently experiencing the same despair, to feel less alone.

Although this period of our life was indeed fraught with sadness and disappointment, I must say all was not negative. I shall never forget those who were willing to support me, among whom two particular examples spring to mind. I am indebted to one of my husband's colleagues who stepped in at the last minute to replace him at a meeting in Rio de Janeiro, so that I was not alone when I suffered an ectopic pregnancy. And then there was one of our best friends who, one day when I was at the depths of despair, gallantly accepted to accompany me on what is today etched in our minds as being a 'legendary' walk in the Bois de Boulogne. It was a walk during which I poured out every last detail of my grief to him, therefore requiring us to do several laps of the Grand Lac!

Neither will I forget the team of doctors – in my eyes true geniuses – who treated me during those long years, without whom we would *never* have had children.

*

When finally I found myself expecting our son, this pregnancy – my third, deemed to be something of a miracle by our doctors (!) – brought its own new batch of complications. However, these complications were easier to bear for the simple reason that everyone – the medical team and my husband and I alike – was under the impression that *this* baby was here to stay.

Naturally, given our track record, things were complicated right to the end.

And even for some time afterwards...

When, at last, our son was born, he looked absolutely perfect to us: a tiny, little, beautifully formed being.

That said, the deafening silence in the delivery room informed us that something was wrong.

Then came the verdict: he was much too small for the term.

I just didn't want to believe it. He looked so very normal. He was, moreover, looking up at me with one eye closed and the other open, as if to give me a little wink of complicity that appeared to say: 'They're all panicking. But don't worry Mummy. You and I both know that it's all going to be okay.'

Sadly, shortly after his birth, our son had to be transferred to a special care baby unit. We just could not believe it. We'd waited so long to get him and already, we were deprived of him! I couldn't stop thinking about the Biblical story of the judgment of Solomon in which the biological mother ultimately accepts to let her newborn go but only because she realises it is her sole chance of saving him.

The period that followed saw us on a constant pendulum swing between a dream fulfilled – that of, at long last, having our very own baby – and the nightmarish thought that we might at any moment lose him.

Then one morning, after many, many angst-ridden, seemingly endless days, the doctors gave us some really good news. Due to a battery of tests, they had managed to eliminate any suspicion of a congenital defect; the cause of the dramatic drop in our son's growth rate towards the end of the pregnancy was insignificant with no long-term consequences. All that remained was for our baby boy to put on some weight and then he could go home.

Sadly, our relief was to be extremely short-lived. That night I had to be re-hospitalised, this time in intensive care, victim of an extremely rare, highly dangerous post-partum syndrome. A large team of medics worked through the night to save me.

Two days later, a doctor entered my room and announced:

'I did everything I could to protect your future because you're still quite young. But you need to know that, given your complications, it's now going to be very difficult for you to have another baby.'

This prognosis struck me as so utterly unfair that I could not help but burst out laughing as I put the following question to him:

'Have you read my file?'

'No, why?'

'Well, if you had, you might just have made the effort to put this bad news to me in a more diplomatic way. You see, the thing is, I had a terrible few years trying to have my first child. But everybody said 'the main thing is to get the machinery going', that once I'd had one child everything would be easier. And now you've just waltzed in to tell me that, in fact, it's going to be quite the opposite.'

'I'm sorry. I didn't know.'

I refrained from saying: 'It's your job to know.' In any case, I couldn't resent him too much. He had, after all, just saved my life. And, besides, there was now another life that mattered so much more than anything else.

*

A few days later, our little family was at long last united; we were, all three of us, at home. From that point on, my husband and I no longer contemplated the future, and what it may or may not hold in store for us, for we simply wanted to enjoy the present. *Carpe diem.*

My overriding memory of this period is one of intense joy. So much so that sometimes I wonder whether, in order to gain access to true happiness, an experience of deep suffering is actually required. Who knows?

Logically, everyone assumed that we would be overprotective parents. In reality, though, it was just the opposite; we turned out to be extremely laid-back! As far as I was concerned, the explanation for this was quite simple: often the arrival of the first child will transform a couple's orderly life into chaos and some find this extremely difficult to deal with. In our case, however, with the arrival of our son came an immense feeling of relief: the tough times were now a thing of the past. So, from then on, everything was actually much easier for us.

Because we were so relaxed, our baby was too. In fact he was quite possibly the most laid-back baby we'd ever come across. He also happened to be the cleanest! We both so wanted to look after him that we would fight over who was to give him his bath. In the end, rather than fighting, we decided that I would bath him every morning and my husband would do the same at night.

Every single aspect of life with our beautiful baby boy seemed amazing to us. We were perfectly prepared for him to keep us up all night – we were even looking forward to it – because general wisdom informed us that *that* was what happened when you became a parent. But – oh, the irony! – very early on, when he was just three weeks old, our wonderful son began sleeping through the night.

So, although we were supposed to be exhausted, in fact we were in fine fettle. In any event, with or without the sleepless nights, no fatigue could ever have been as bad as that which we had experienced during our struggle of the previous years.

In short, these blissful times were proof that every instant of that struggle had been completely worth it. In terms of physical hardship, I had been through the equivalent of ten pregnancies to have just one child but, now, our intense joy was giving it all a meaning: our reward for all the trials and tribulations was a form of happiness that appeared to be increased tenfold in relation to that which we might have known had we had our baby in more normal circumstances.

It was, therefore, not long before the following idea began to creep into our minds: what if we were to multiply this happiness by two...?

*

As time went by, it became apparent that the undiplomatic doctor had in fact been right: our desire to expand our family was turning out to be very difficult.

When, after three years, I learned that yet more surgery would be required if I wanted to have another child, it just seemed so unfair; to have my first child, I'd already been through three operations and three pregnancies – not to mention the countless appointments, invasive examinations and all the various treatments. Furthermore, I was under the distinct impression that I had long since depleted the supply of energy I could possibly devote to this cause; I no longer had any left to give.

And yet, I needed to find just a little bit more. I had no choice but to do so. We had to give it one last chance to avoid any subsequent regrets.

✳

In the recovery room, I heard the doctor exclaim:

'It went really well. In three months' time, you'll be pregnant!'

We did better than that, though. Two months later, I had a sneaking suspicion it had already happened. Initially I said nothing, for fear of giving false hope.

When, finally, I had confirmation of this good news, I called my husband who – blissfully unaware of my reason for phoning him – said to me:

'I can't talk now. I'm in a meeting... and it's really important.'

'Leave the meeting. What I have to say to you is very important too.'

In the face of my insistence, he left the room fearing bad news. Upon his return, he could barely contain his smile.

We were indeed over the first hurdle but the road was long and fraught, once again, with major complications.

My pregnancy was immediately classified as 'high risk' meaning that I was to be monitored particularly closely. I was also under strict doctor's orders to lie down, with my feet up, for several interminably long weeks. Once again, some people came out with comments that would leave me reeling with disbelief: 'There's no need to make such a meal of it. You're not ill, you know. You're just pregnant.' But, as far as I was concerned, only one opinion was of any real consequence – that of the medical profession – whose view was this: 'We are going to do all we can to get it right. But the fact remains that this pregnancy is extremely precarious and potentially very dangerous. We cannot, therefore, afford to make the slightest mistake.' In any case, I no longer had the energy to explain my very real (and most certainly not imaginary) problems to such self-opinionated people. Thus it was that I coolly deleted, from my address book, the name of any person who took the liberty of saying such insensitive things and retreated into a cocoon of self-protection into which only those who were prepared to show compassion and understanding were invited.

*

Obviously, there was absolutely no way I could impart the details of my long road to motherhood to the lawyer who was currently standing before me at the cab rank. I would, however, so have loved to be able to explain to him exactly why the mere fact of being allowed, at long last, to stand up was actually making me feel ecstatically happy; contrary to what he thought, I was, in reality, savouring every last second because to be standing there – a few days before I was due to give birth to our second child – constituted, as far as I was concerned, the best possible proof of my personal triumph.

*

One week later, our daughter was born.

In view of my case history – contained in a file the size of a large encyclopaedia (!) – an army of medical staff assembled in the delivery room, 'just in case', especially for the event. Among them, I counted an obstetrician, a paediatrician, a surgeon, an anaesthetist, a midwife and at least two nurses!

Fortunately, it all went swimmingly with the result that just two hours after our arrival at the clinic, I was already holding our perfect little baby in my arms.

She was the most beautiful girl in the world. Quite an incredible feat, when you think about it, given that four years earlier I had also managed to give birth to the most beautiful boy of the entire planet!

Yes, you've guessed it. Just like the vast majority of parents, we were utterly besotted with our newborn baby and therefore not remotely objective.

A few days later, upon my discharge from the maternity clinic, my husband took his annual holiday. In light of my previous post-partum complications, I was forbidden to travel for some time so we spent the next three weeks enjoying *la dolce vita* at home, in Paris. Every afternoon, we would all go to a local park so as not to disrupt our son's routine. He would thus spend hours playing with his friends in the sandpit, while his little sister slept peacefully in the calm surroundings of her pram that we naturally parked in the shade. In the evenings, when the air became cooler, we would all go for a stroll in the neighbourhood before sitting down to dinner on an open-air restaurant terrace, our daughter by our side in her pram or in our arms when necessary.

We were so proud of our little family, blissfully happy.

Naturally, the books I'd bought for my stay in the maternity clinic were to remain unopened for many months to come. Just *what* had I been thinking?

That said it was of little consequence now. The books could wait, as could the passage explaining the meaning of '*le choix du roi*', for I was currently experiencing the king's choice first-hand and it was truly wonderful. And, besides, I was content merely to contemplate this bag of books because it would remind me of my moving exchange, just a few days prior to giving birth, with the business lawyer in the cab rank.

⋆

As I write these lines it occurs to me that, to this day, I would be hard-pressed to explain precisely what it was about this business lawyer's considerate attitude that left such a mark on me, and an apparently indelible mark at that. Was it because his behaviour was a shining example of the delicate way in which people generally treat pregnant women? Indeed, perfect strangers will go out of their way to show kindness and respect towards us when we are expecting a baby. And, I freely admit, each time I received such treatment it would leave me feeling deeply moved because here was yet more proof that I was experiencing *the* most amazing act we can ever hope to accomplish on this planet: that of giving life.

On a more general note, one thing that particularly strikes me about my exchange with this business lawyer is the idea that we can never really gauge the true extent to which our words will affect others. To take my case, for example, never could I possibly have imagined that simply by saying a taxi smelled of smoke, I would actually galvanise a cabdriver into ditching his habit, literally overnight. In turn, that same cabdriver could not possibly have known that this book – for many years a mere idea in my head – would see the light of day as a result of his comments.

As for my encounter with the business lawyer, I believe (if ever I were to bump into him again) that he would be genuinely surprised to learn just how touched I was by his kindness towards me. So very touched in fact that many years later I find myself writing about it here. I'm sure he would tell me that his behaviour had been perfectly normal in the circumstances. But then normal is such a relative concept, isn't it? And in the case in point, that which was normal for him, ended up transforming for me, the relatively banal act of queuing in a cab rank into a truly memorable mini-slice of life.

✶

Traditionally, the best is for last. And this story is no exception because there is a charming conclusion to this encounter that I have yet to narrate...

After a good fifteen minutes' waiting – during which the business lawyer's level of frustration scaled dizzy heights – a solitary taxi arrived.

Turning to me, the poor man revealed the deep anxiety this situation was causing him – etched as it was all over his face.

Once again, I endeavoured to reassure him as to my wellbeing.

'Do take the taxi. I feel fine, really I do. There's absolutely no problem.'

'Thank you so much, *Madame*. You're most kind. I'm extremely ill-at-ease with this but, like I said, my meeting is important and I'm already horribly late.'

'Go ahead and take it. And I wish you all the best for your meeting!'

'I hope it all goes well for you too. I'm quite sure you'll have a very beautiful baby. Be sure to cherish every moment. They grow up so fast!'

Once in the taxi, he shot me one last extremely anxious look.

Naturally, he could not know that the problem was just about to be resolved.

He was on the point of closing the door when quite suddenly I noticed another taxi approaching.

'*Monsieur*, turn around. Take a look behind you!'

Visibly relieved, he flashed me a wide smile before, at long last, setting off for his meeting.

As for me, with a spring in my step, I got into the next cab – thrilled to have crossed the path of this veritable gentleman.

And it was in this happy frame of mind that I sat down to enjoy my journey home, across *the* most beautiful city in the world, delighting in the idea that this cab ride might just become the subject of yet another taxi tale from Paris…